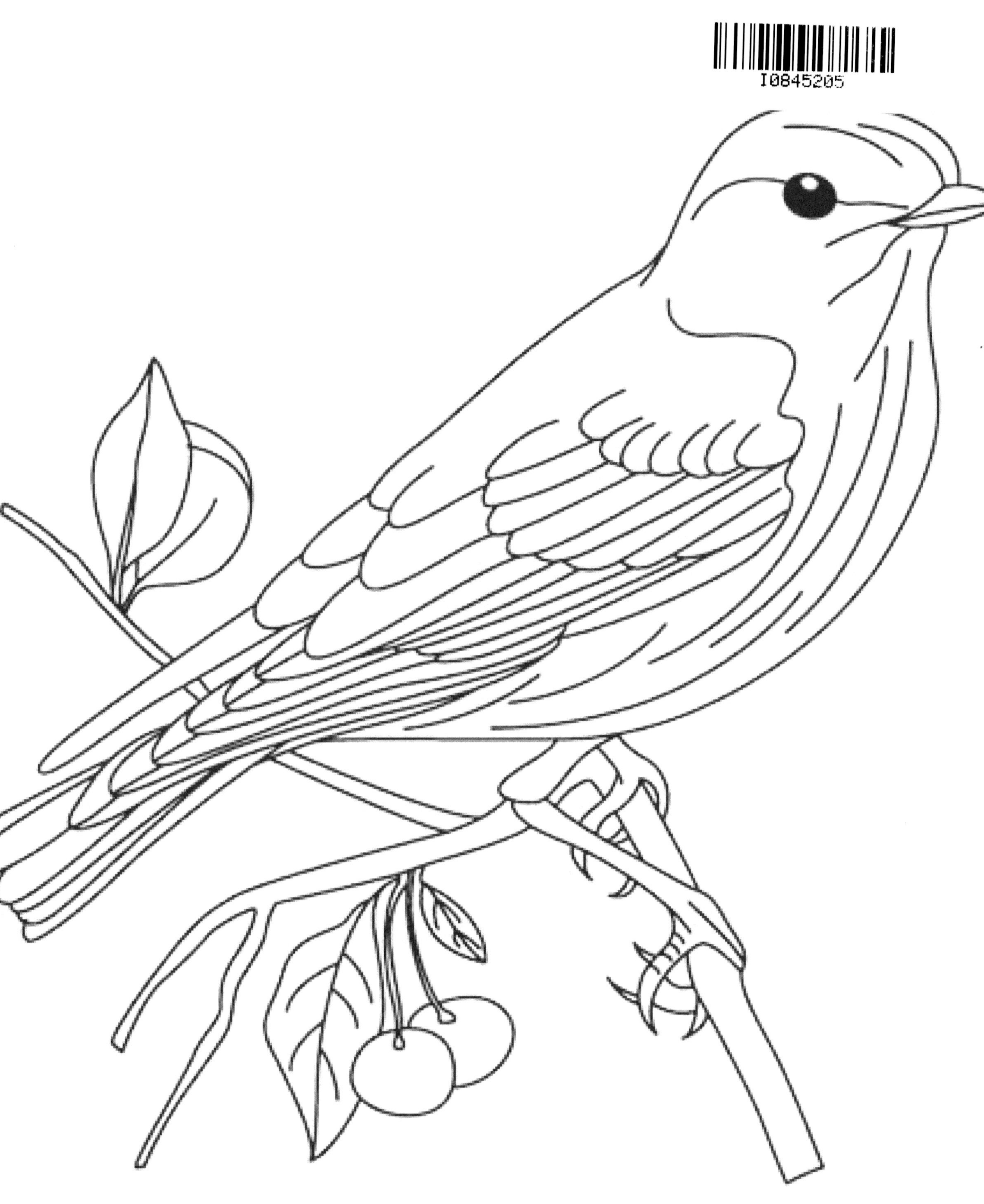

I0845205

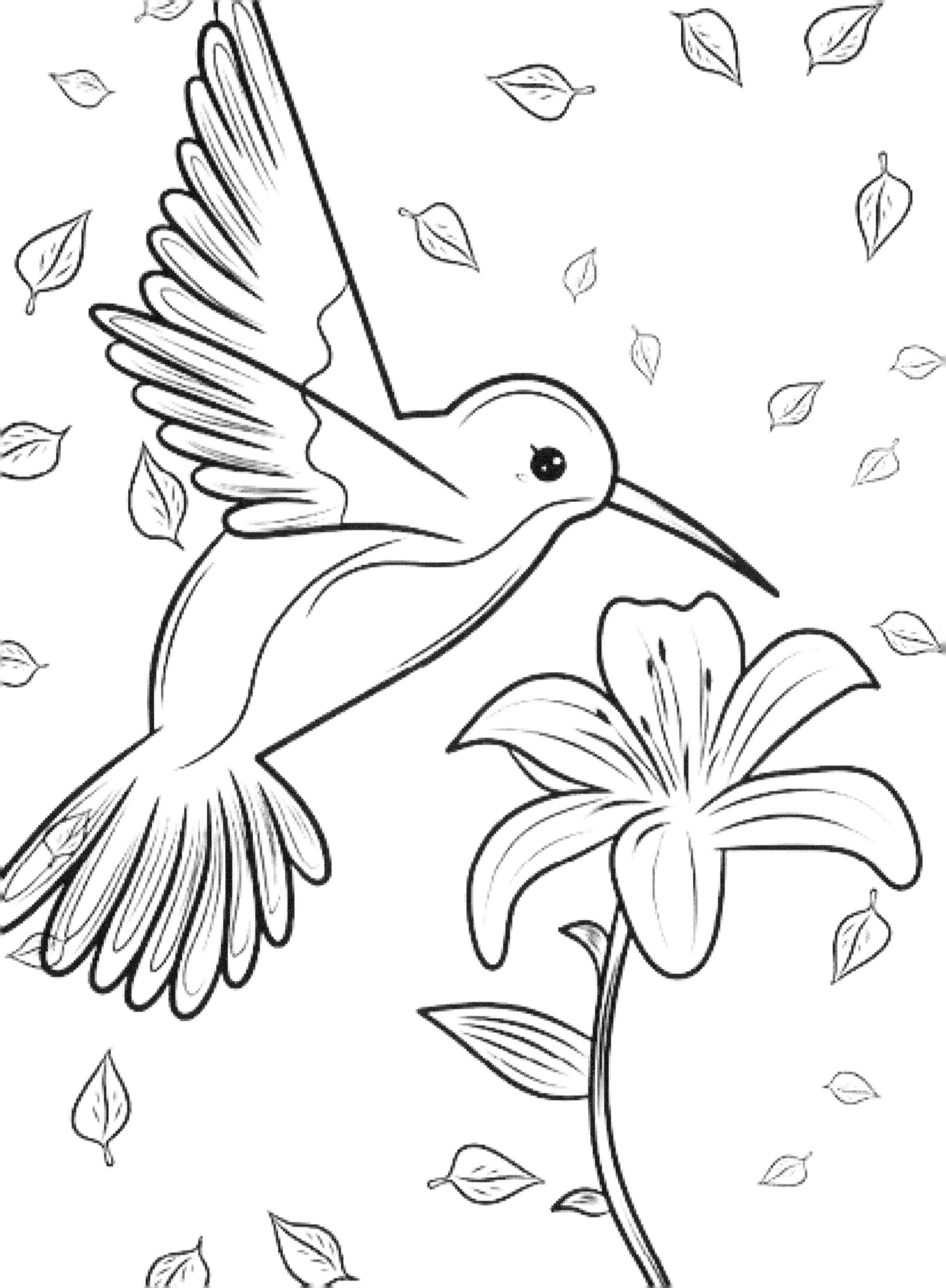

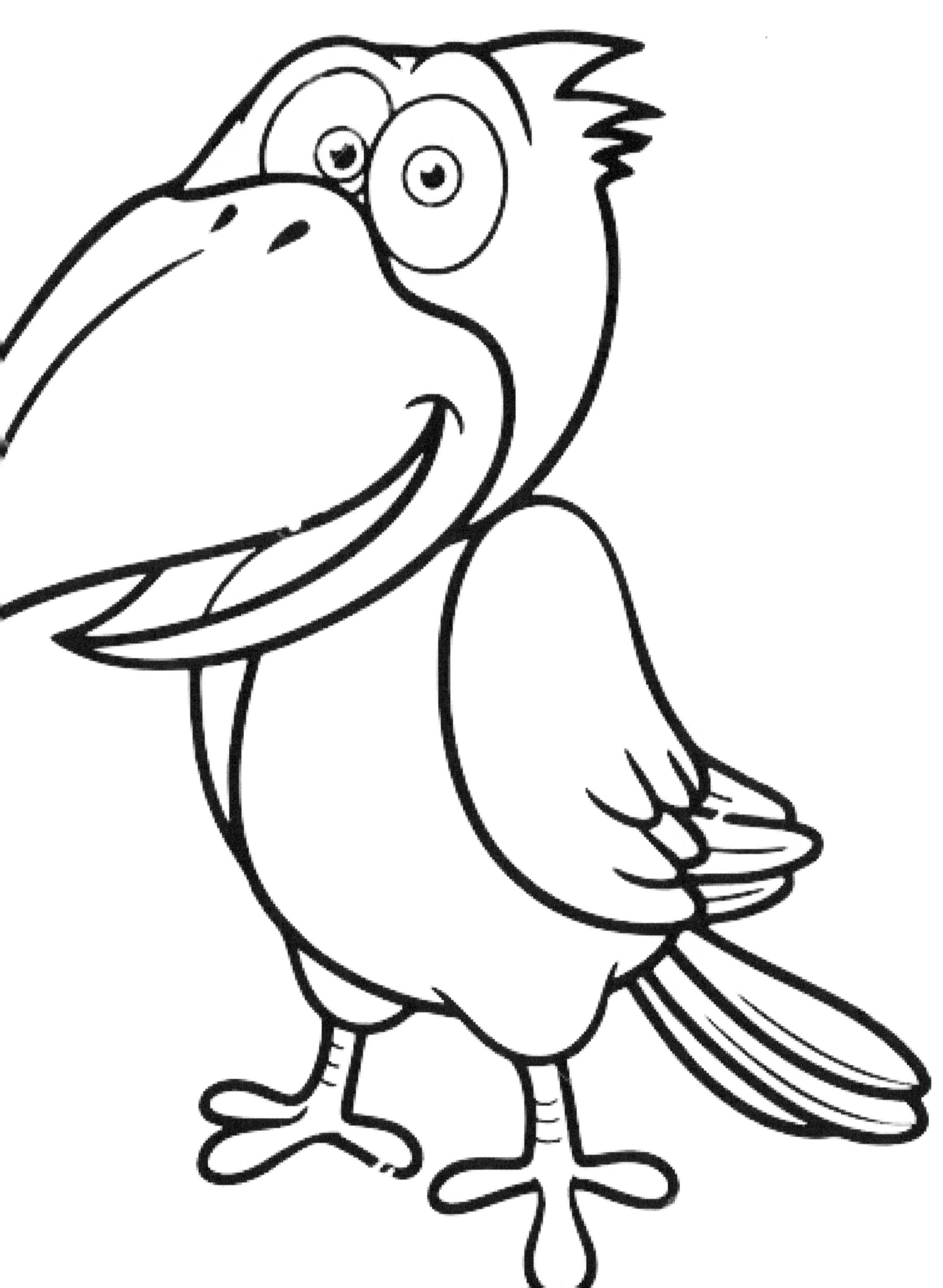

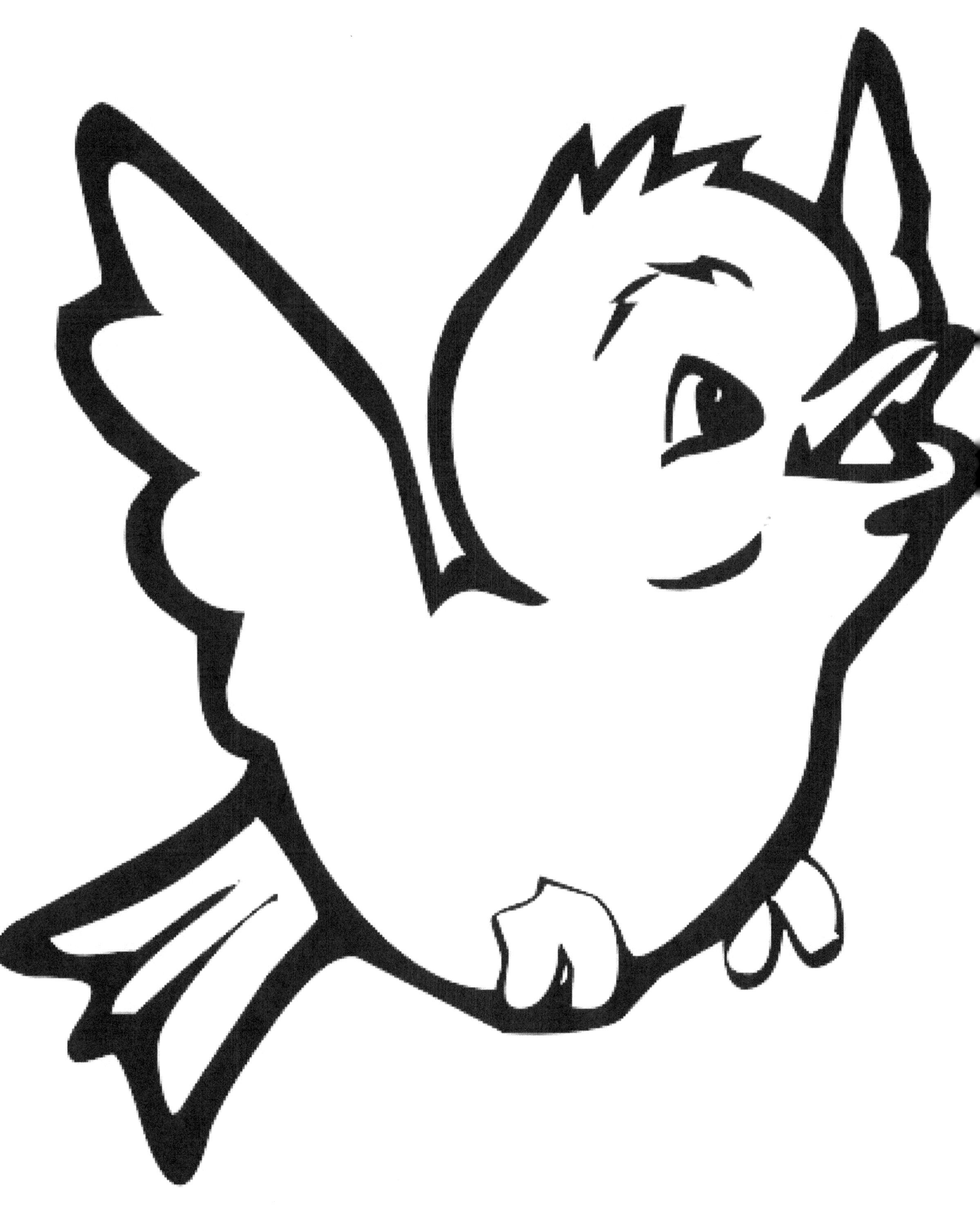

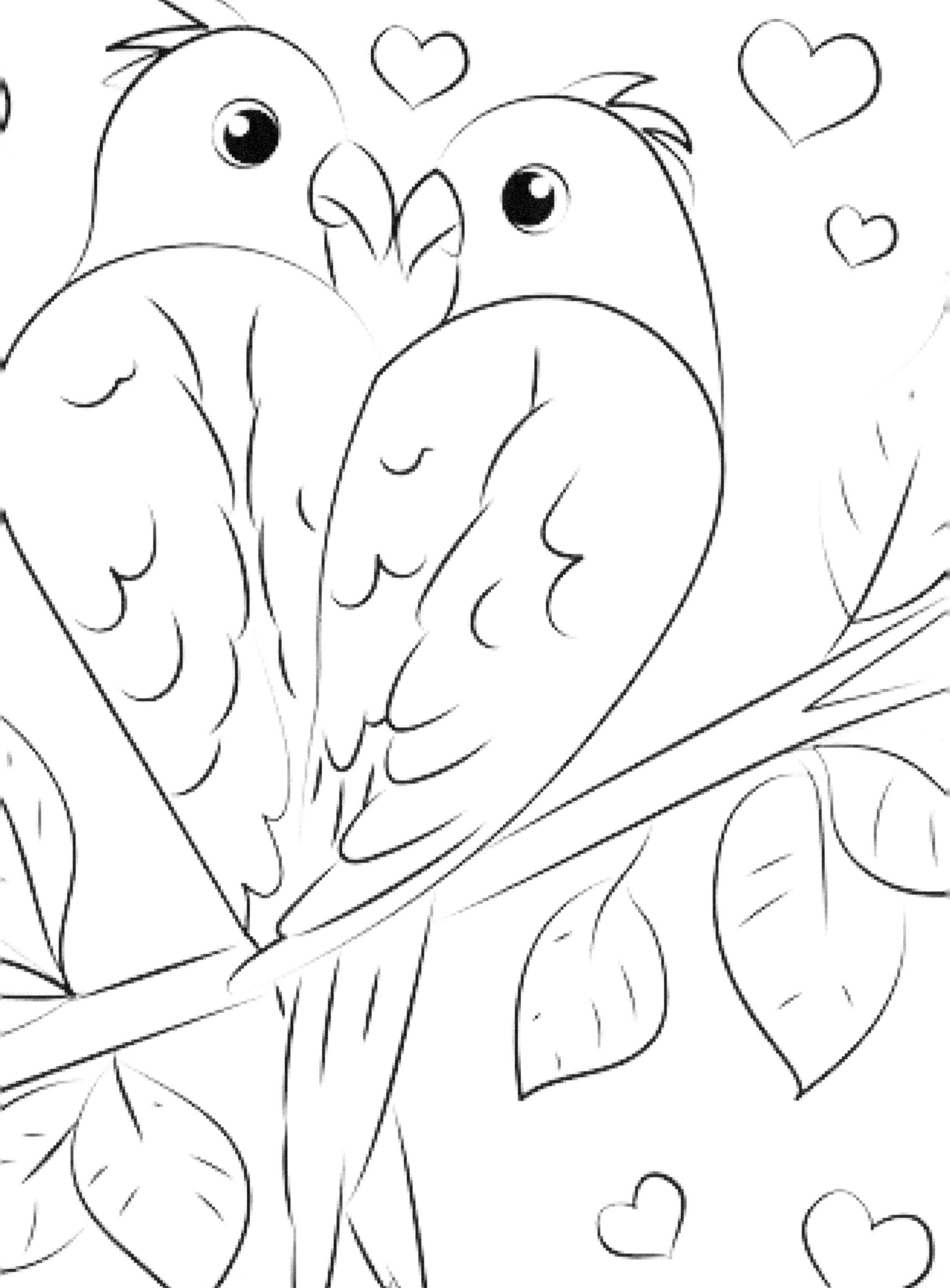

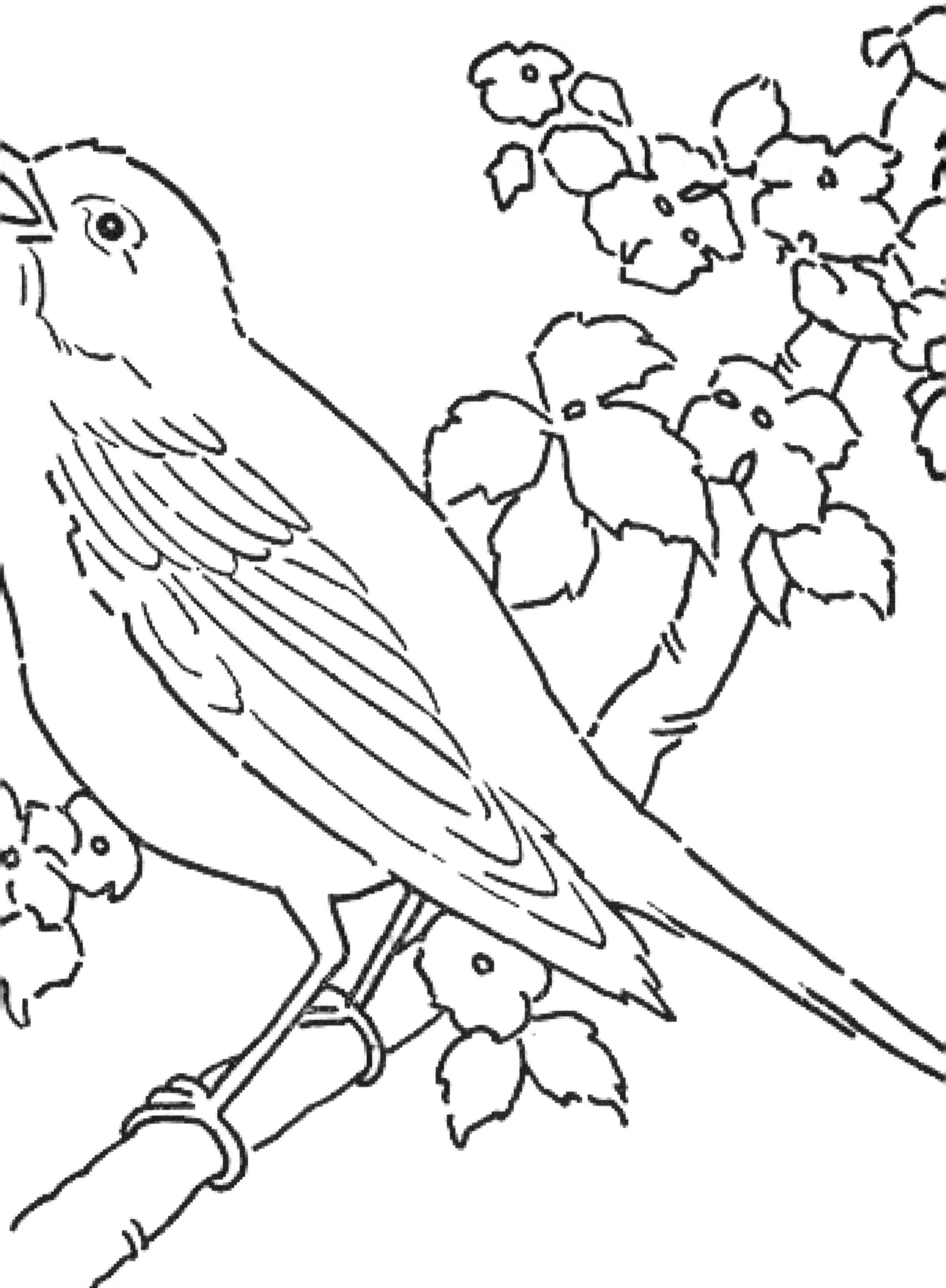

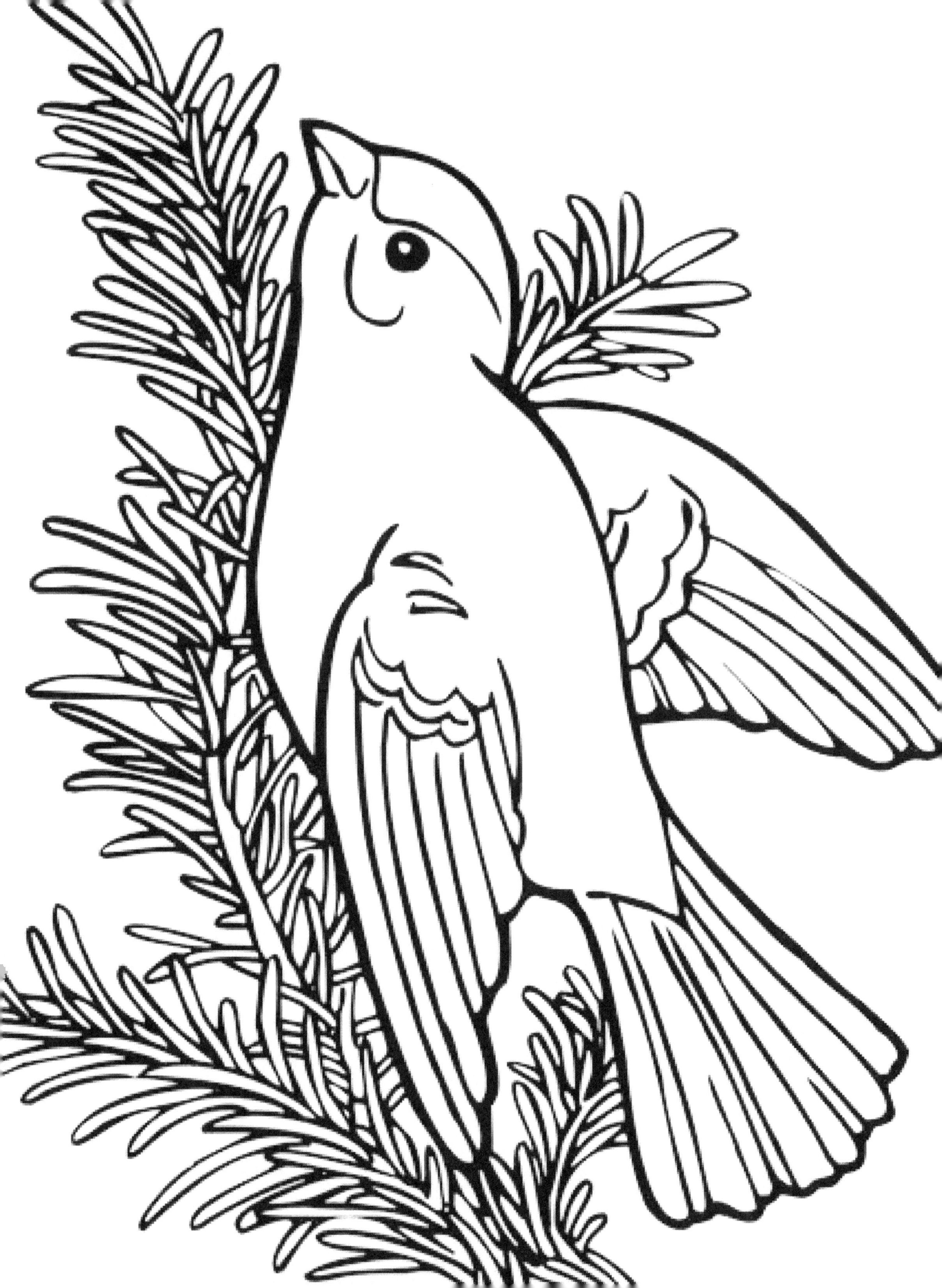

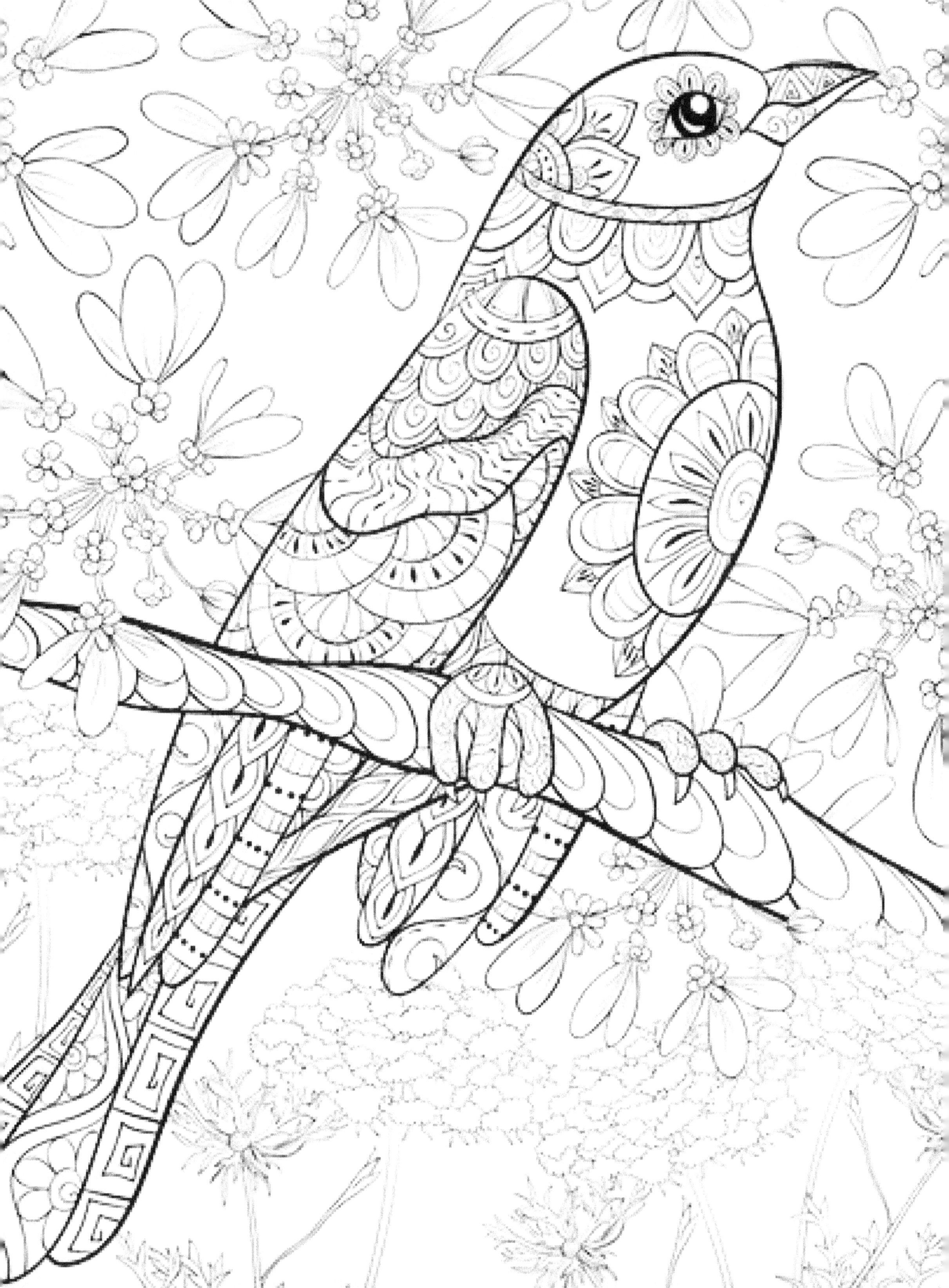

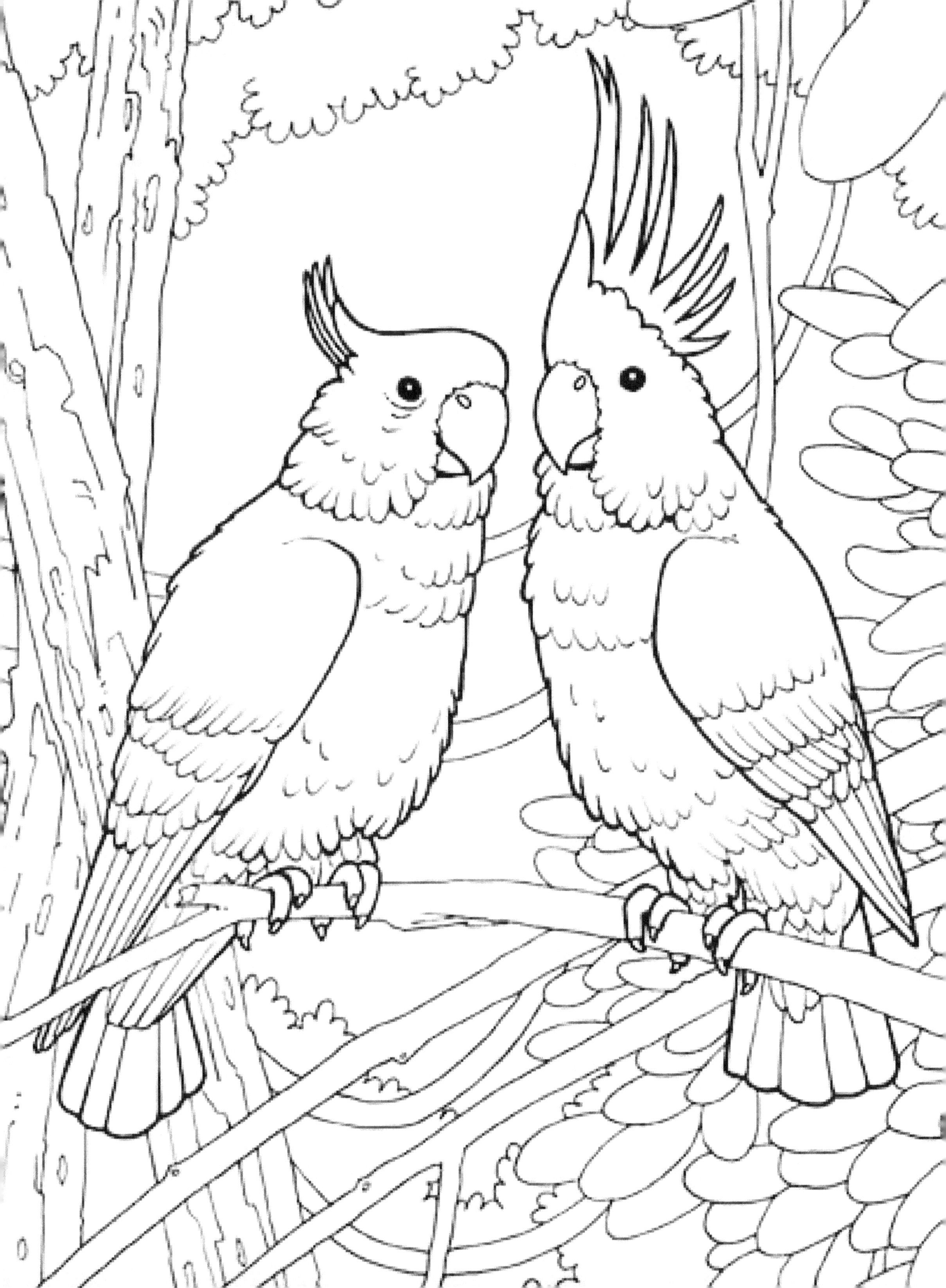

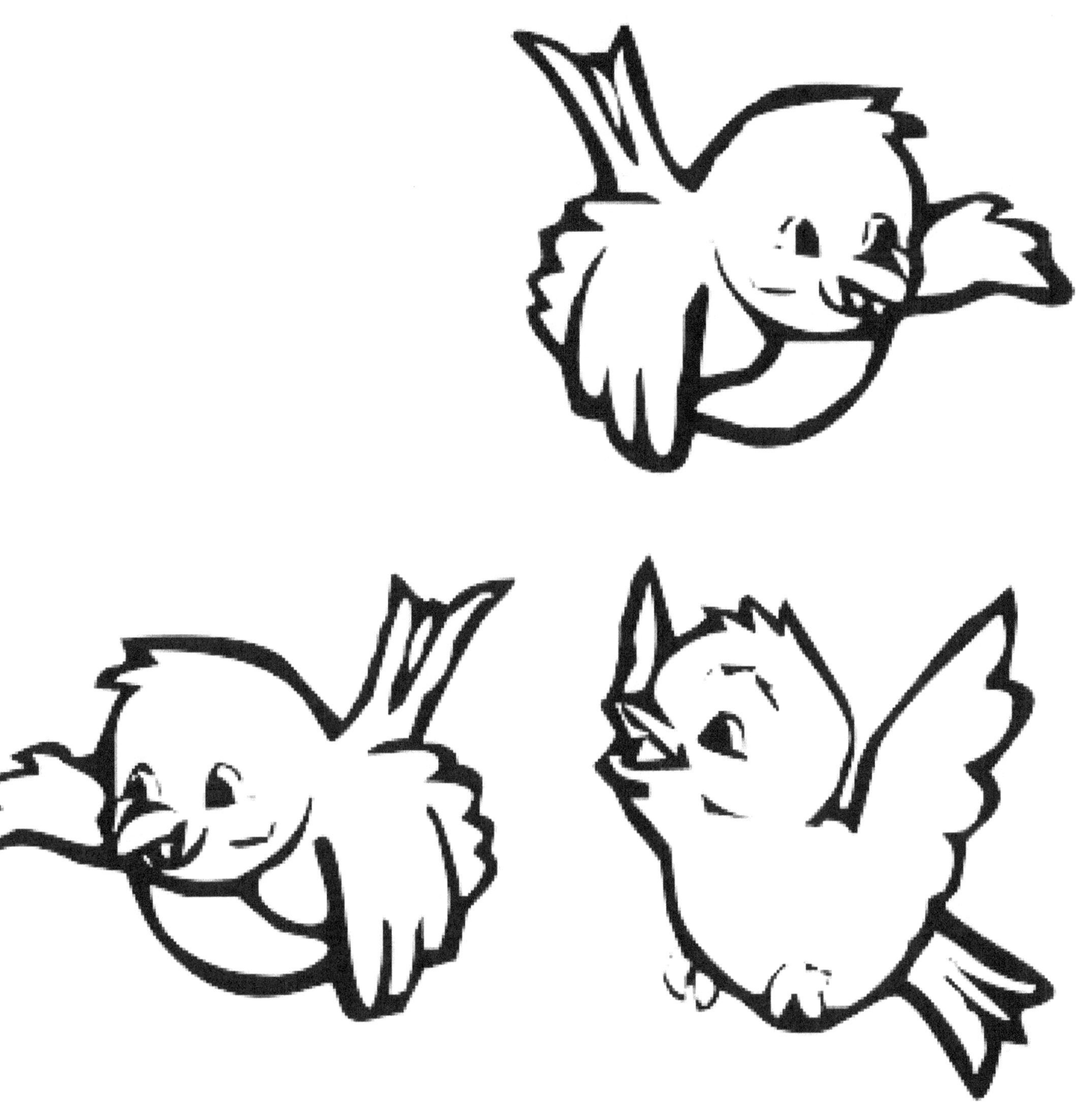

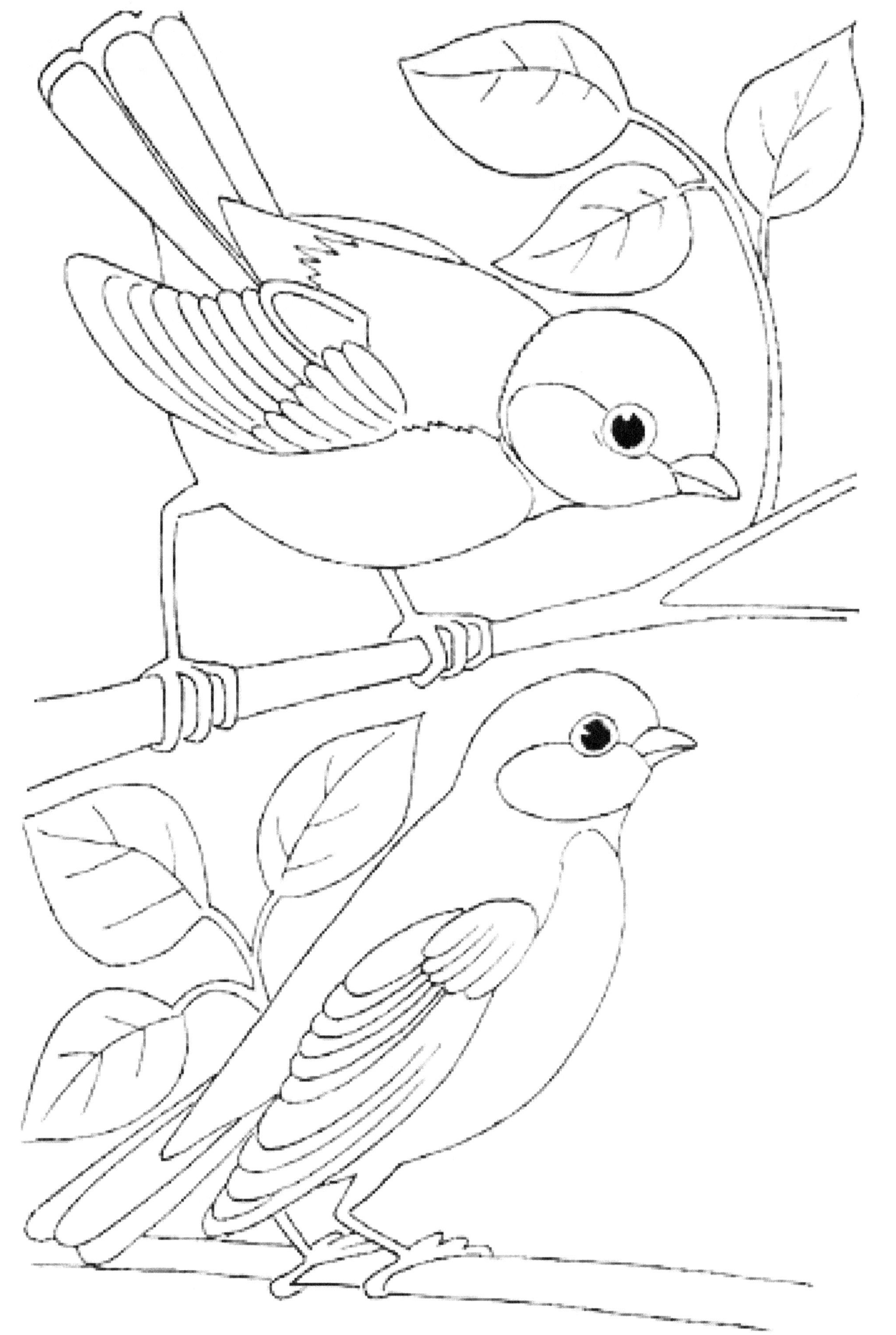

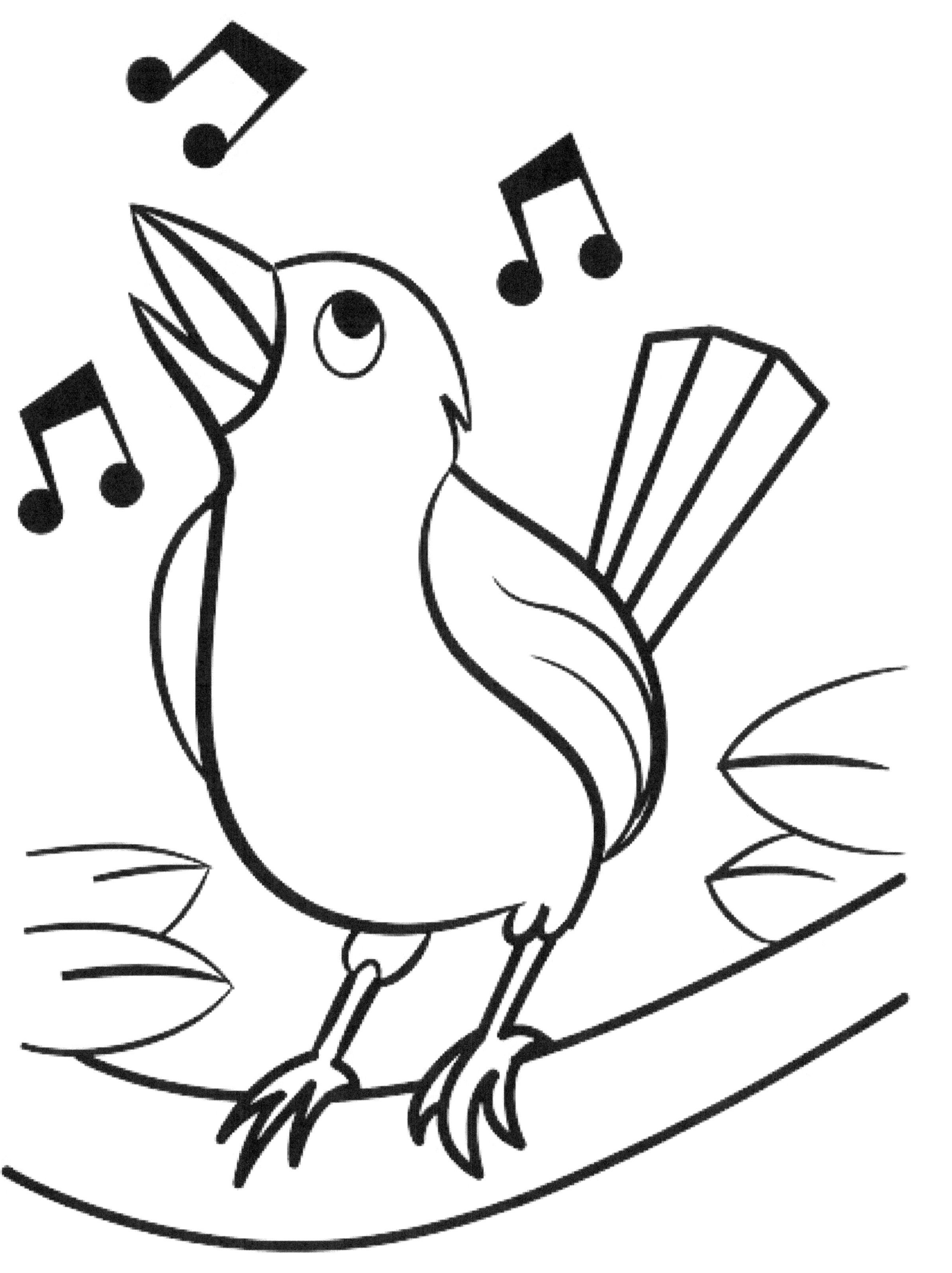

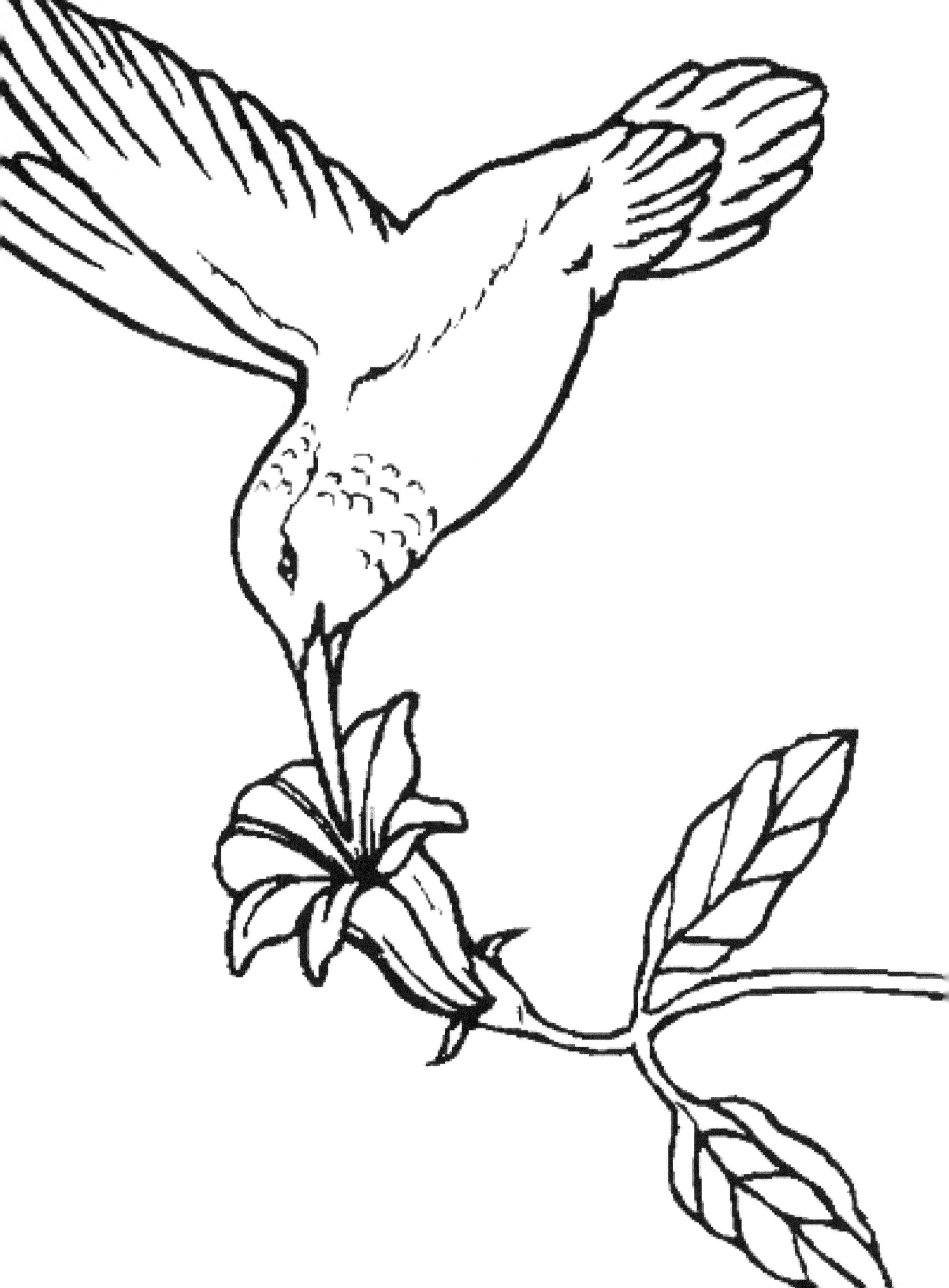

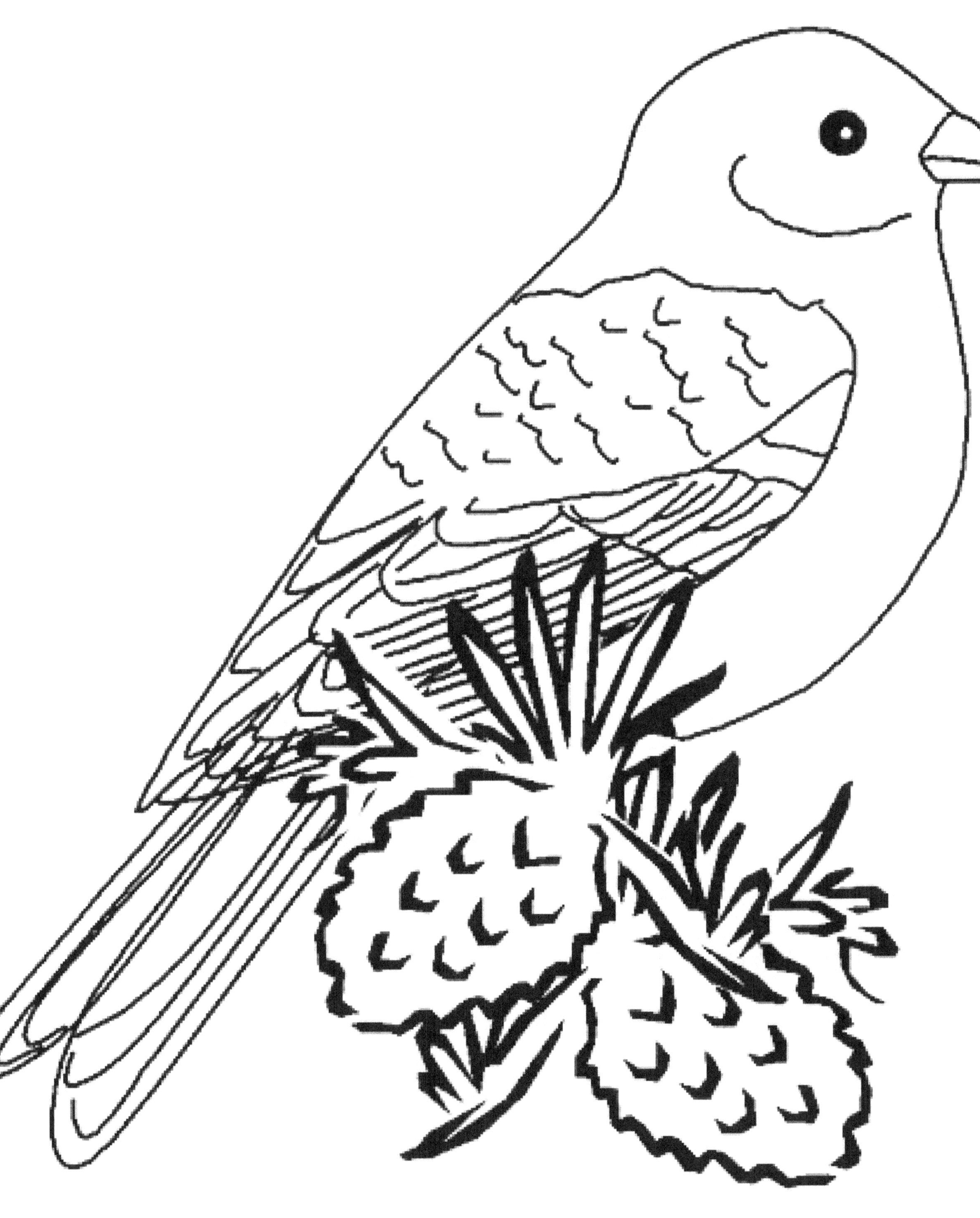

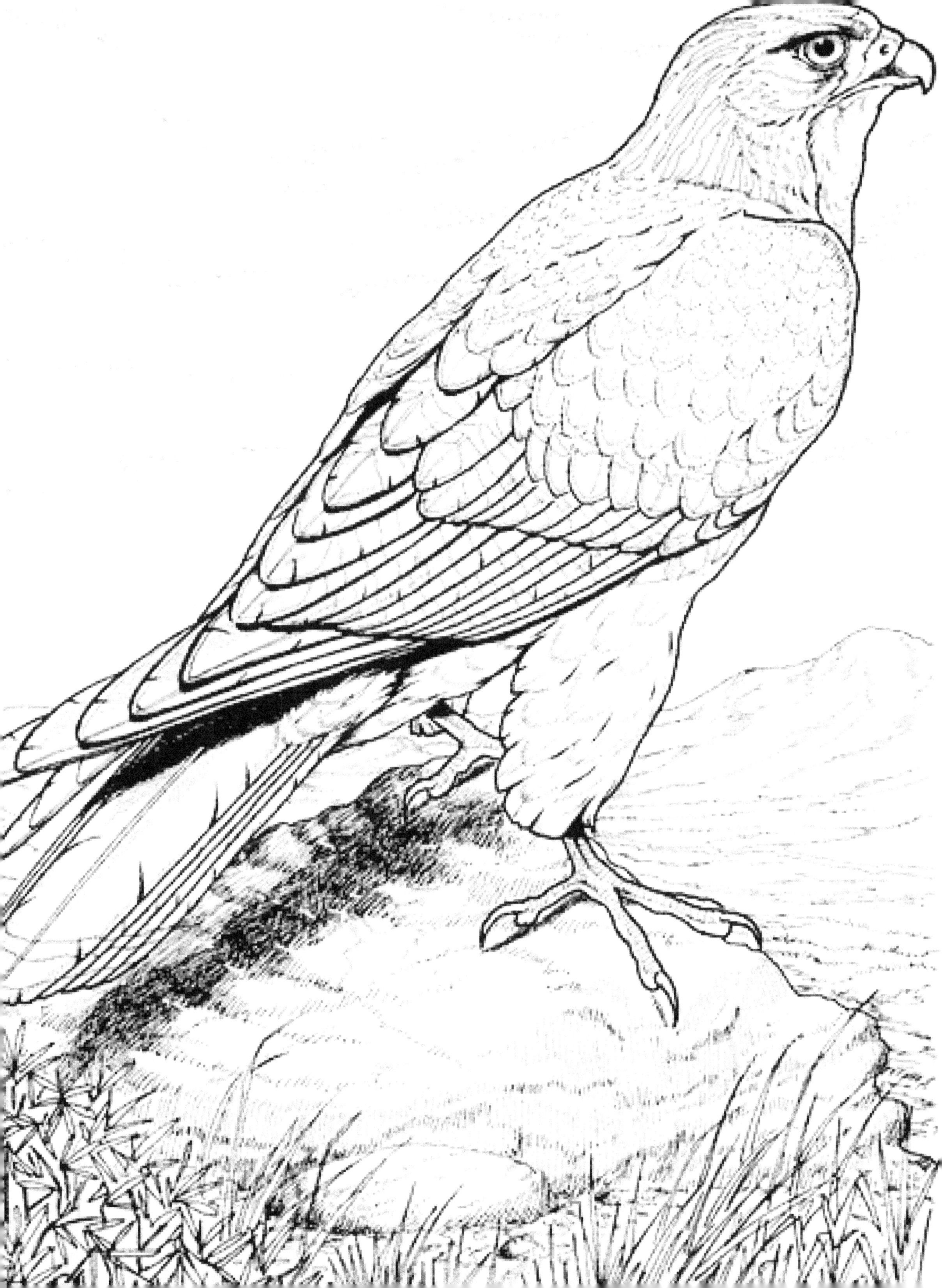

blue bird

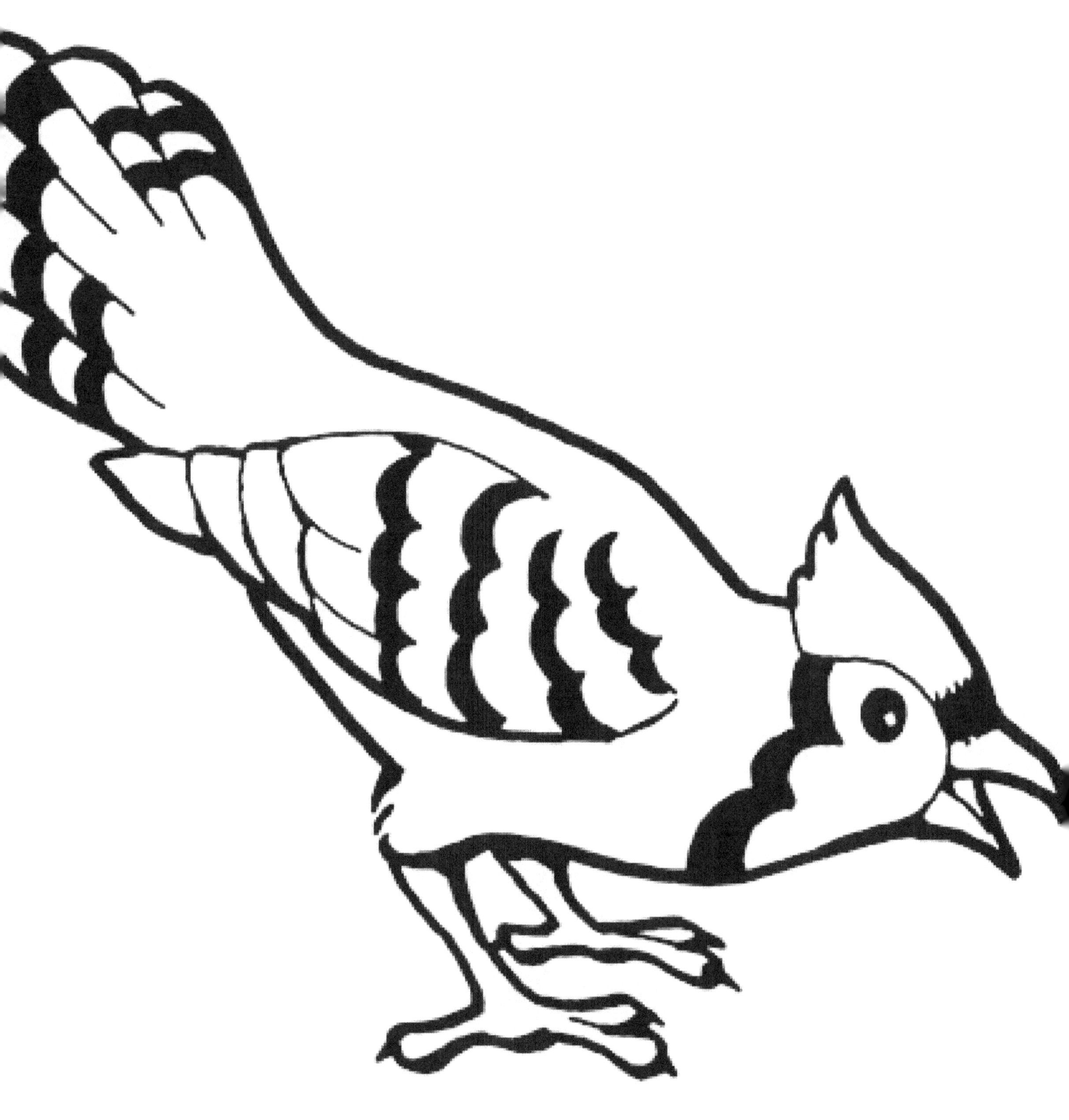

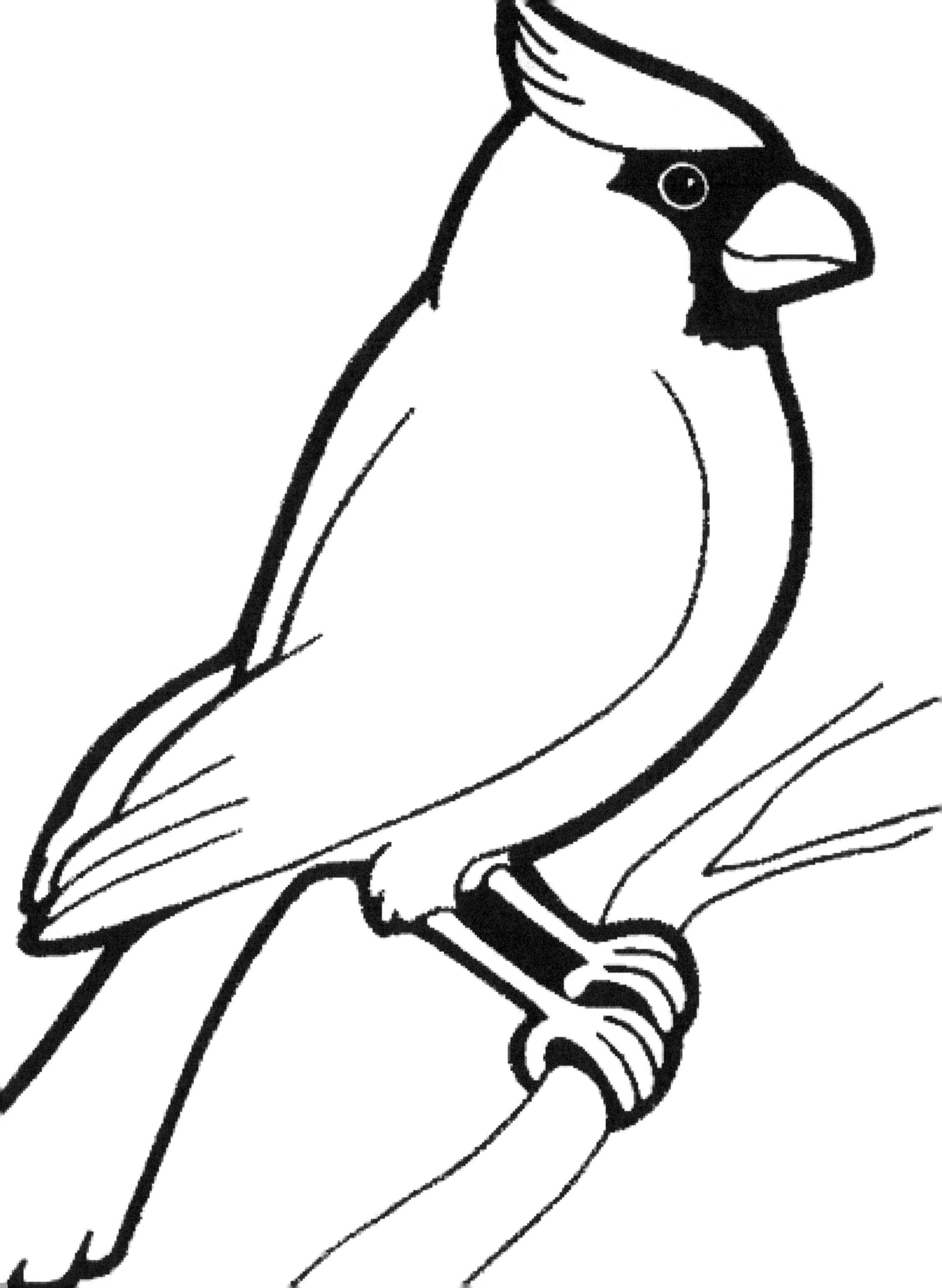

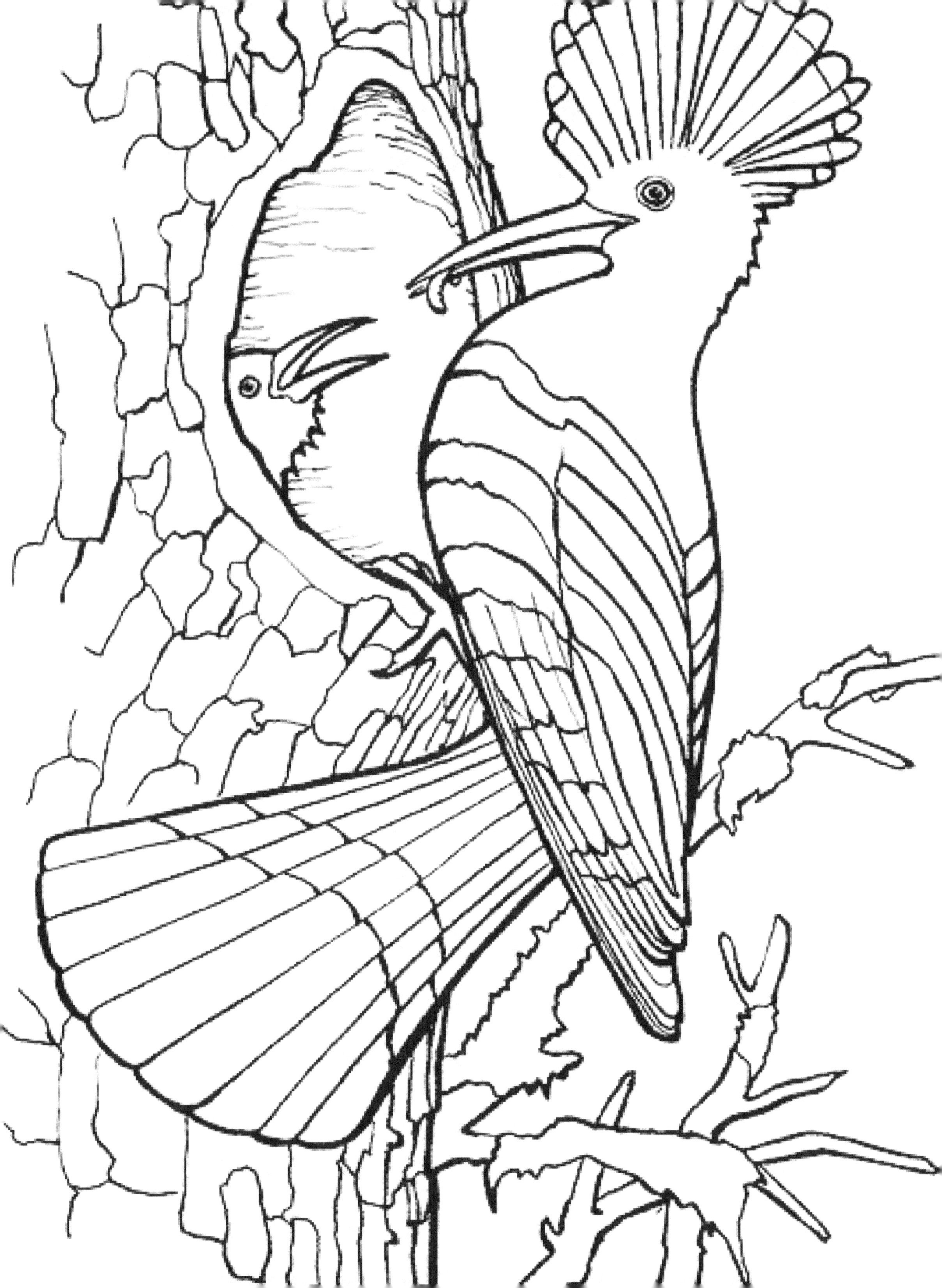

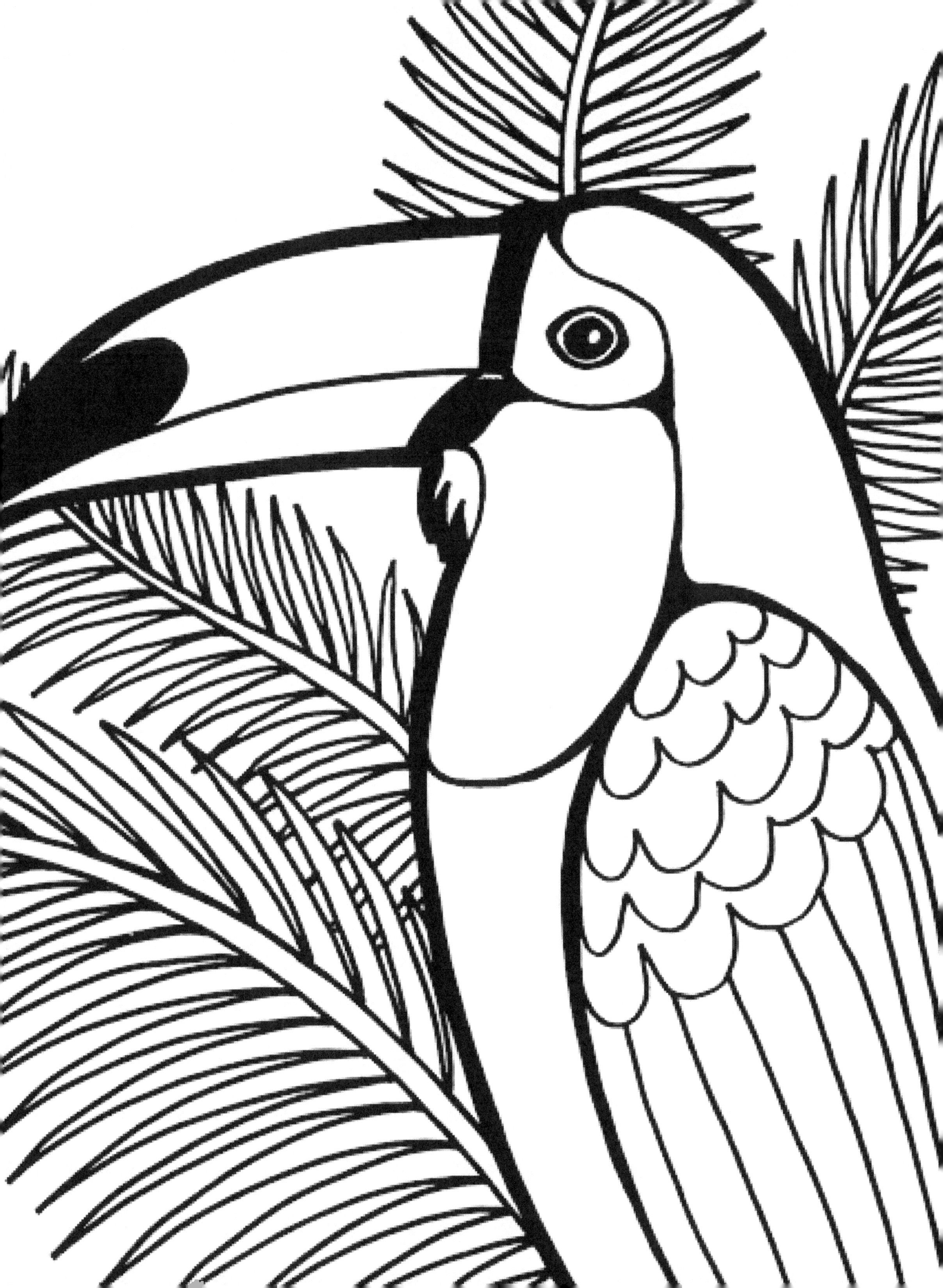

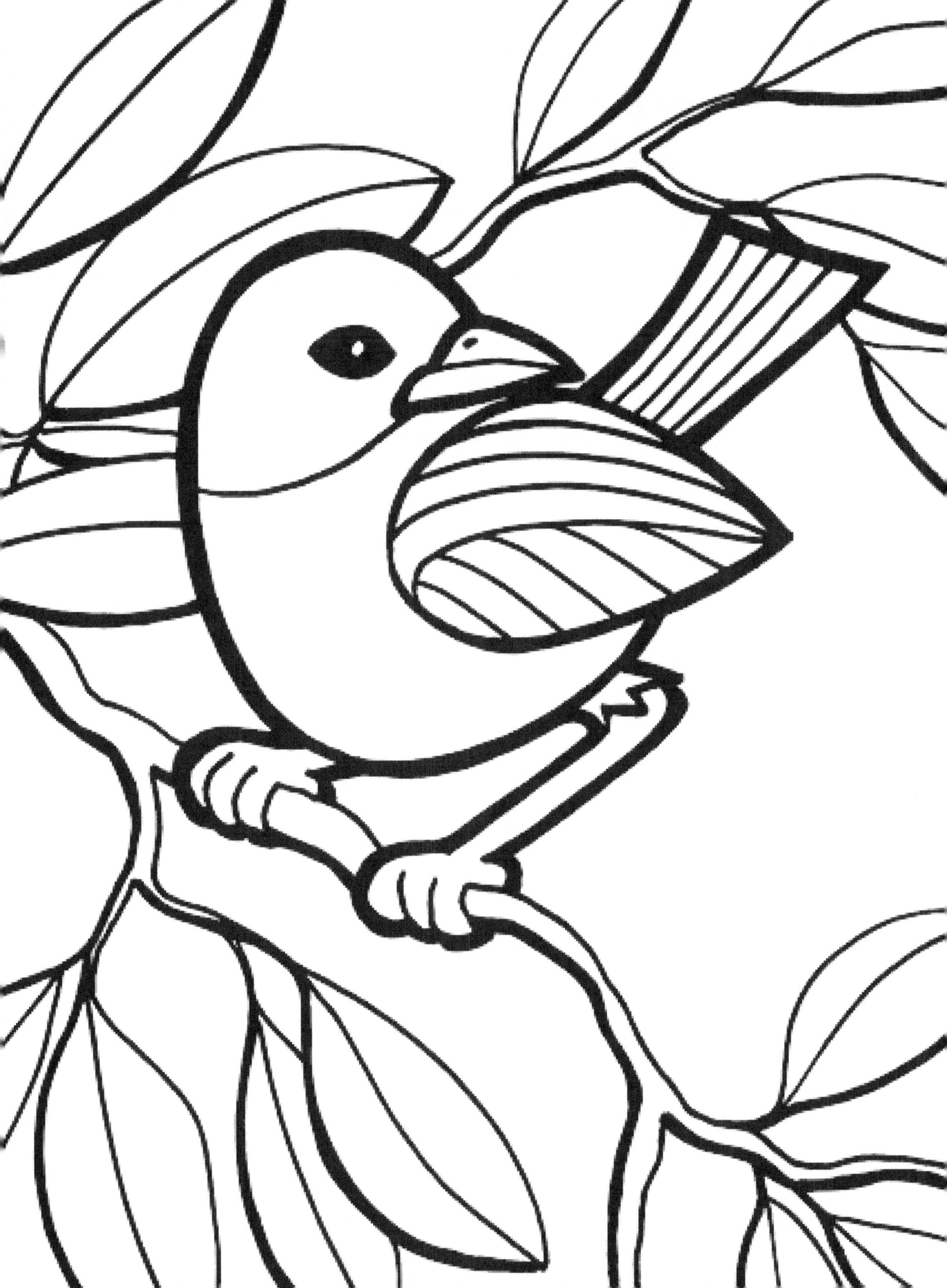

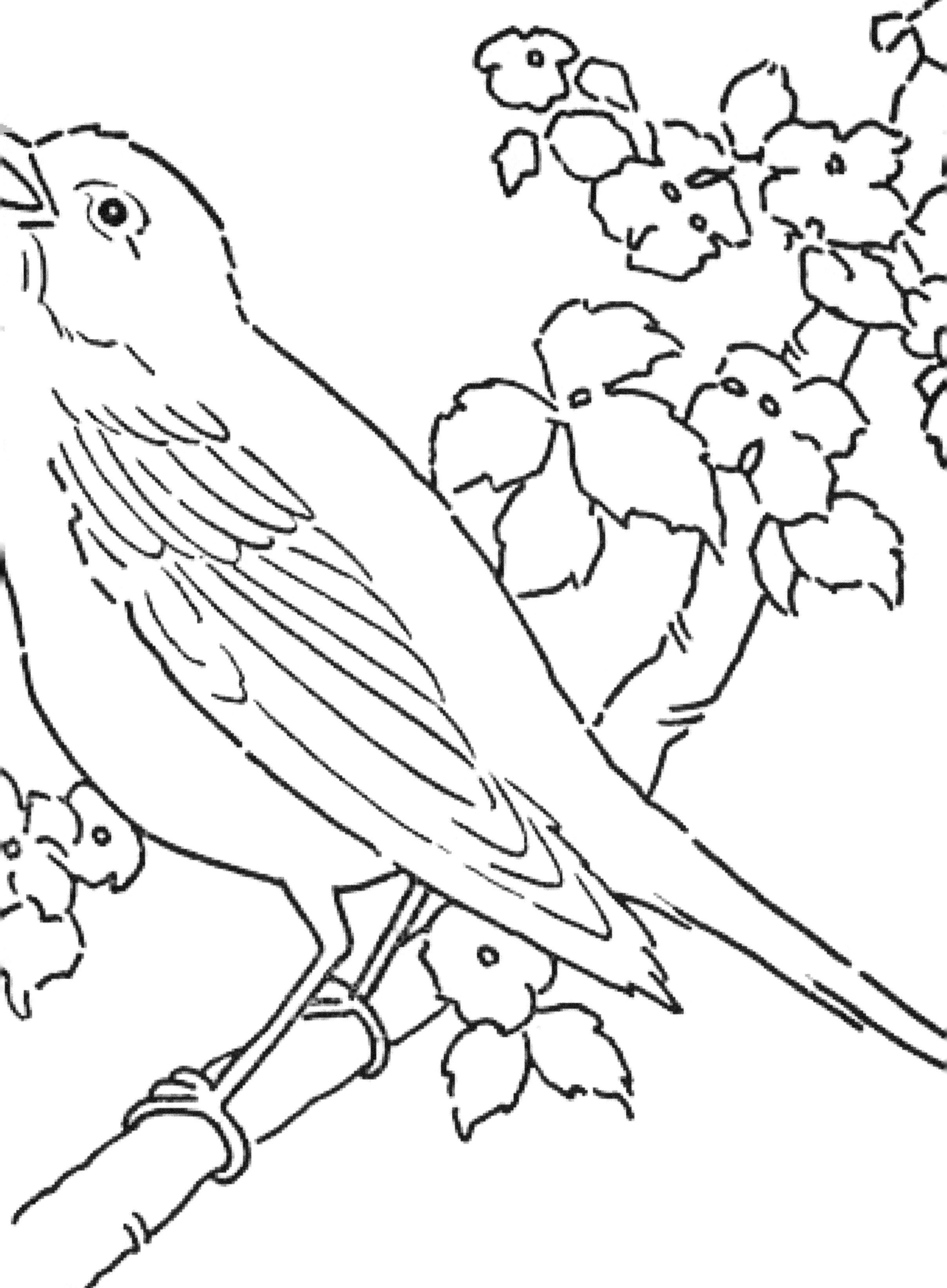

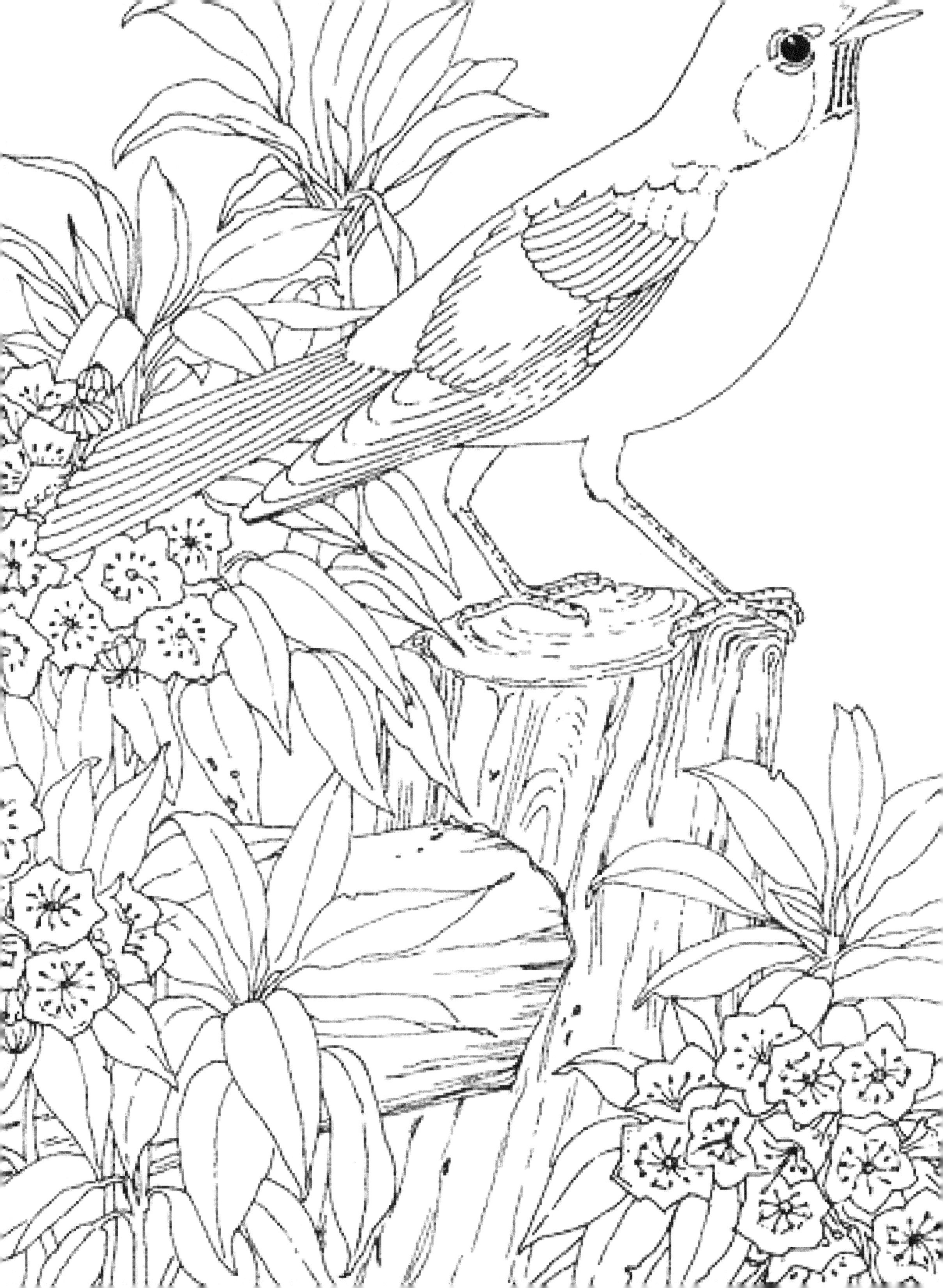

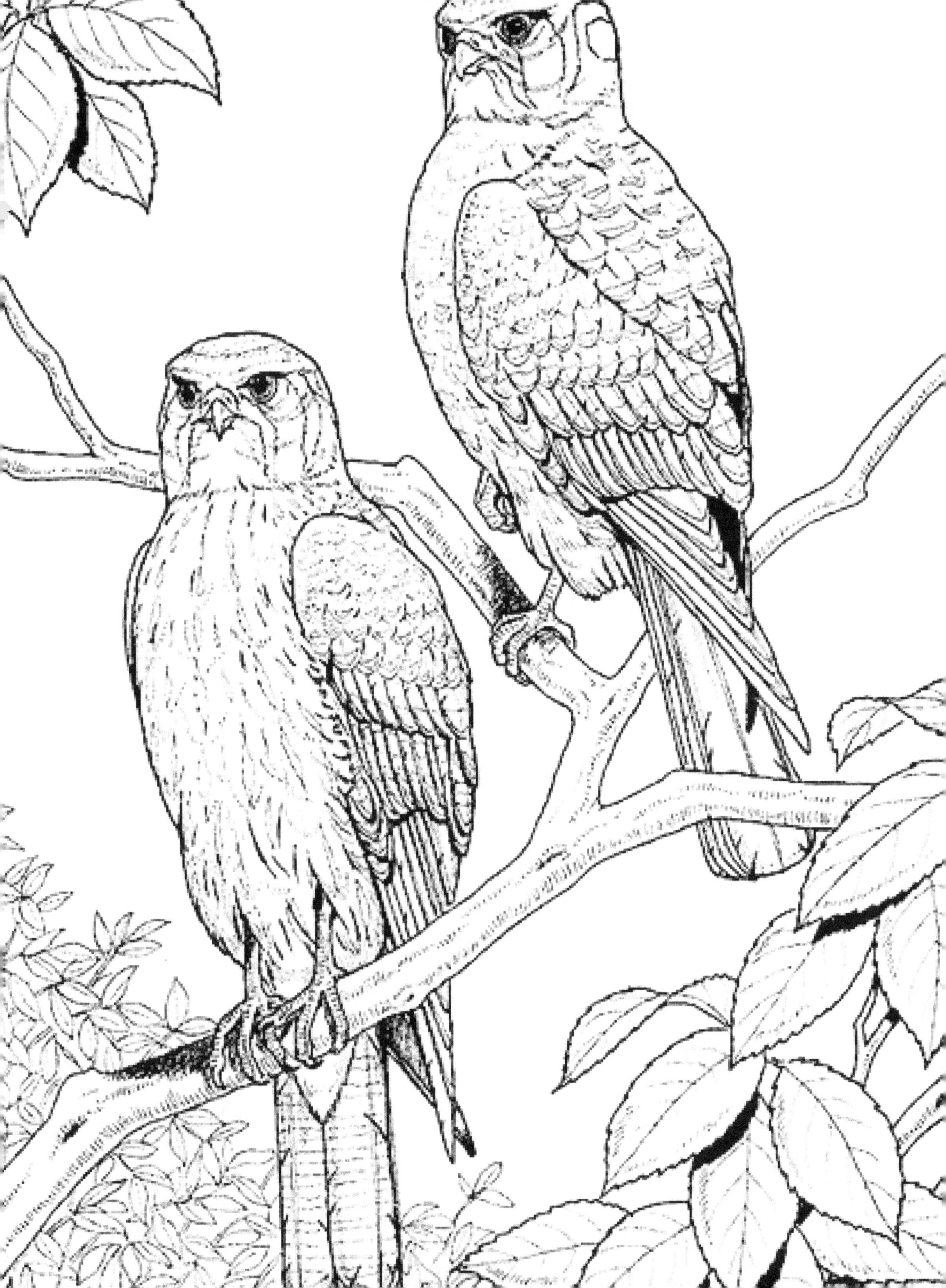

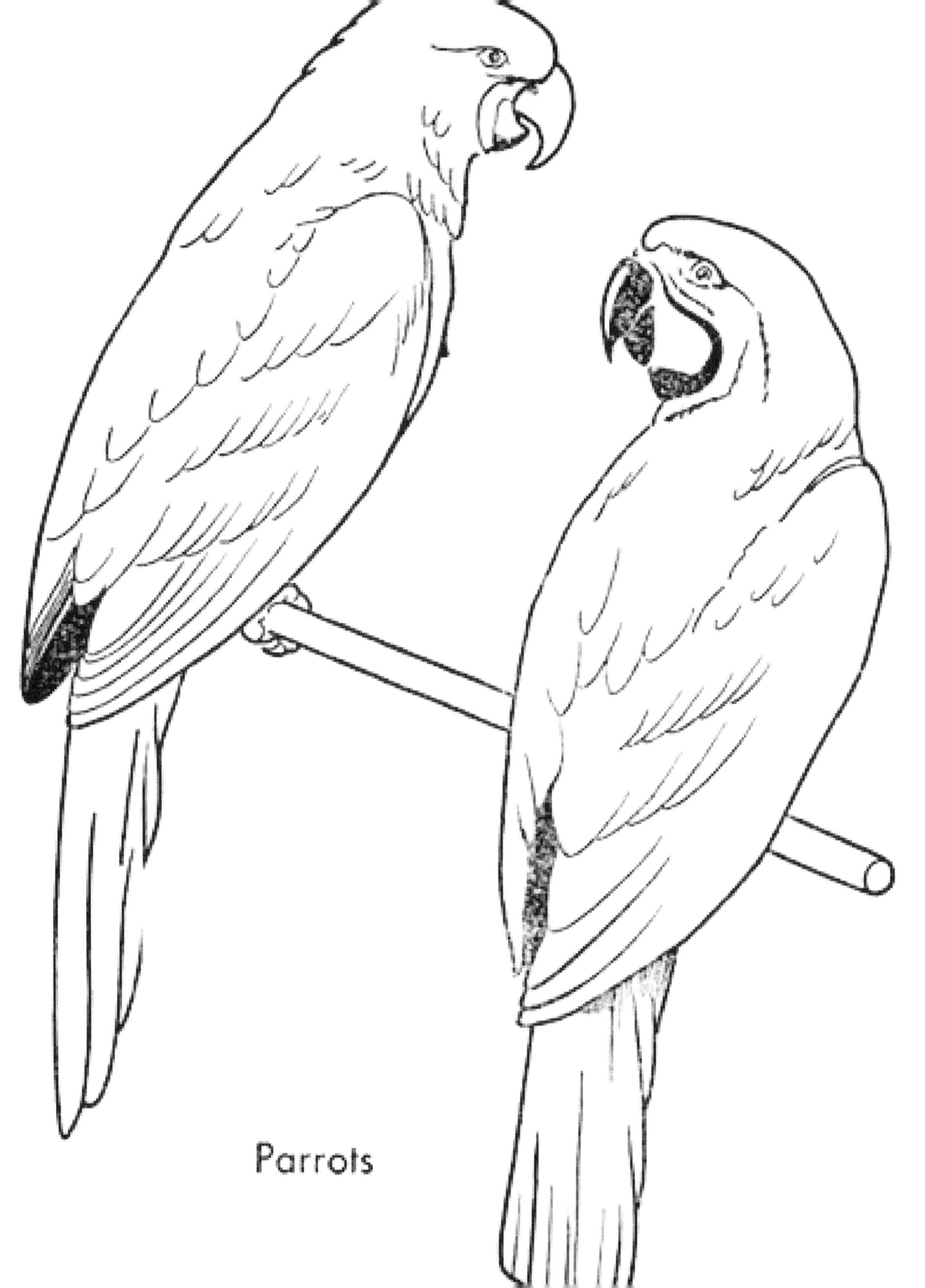

Parrots

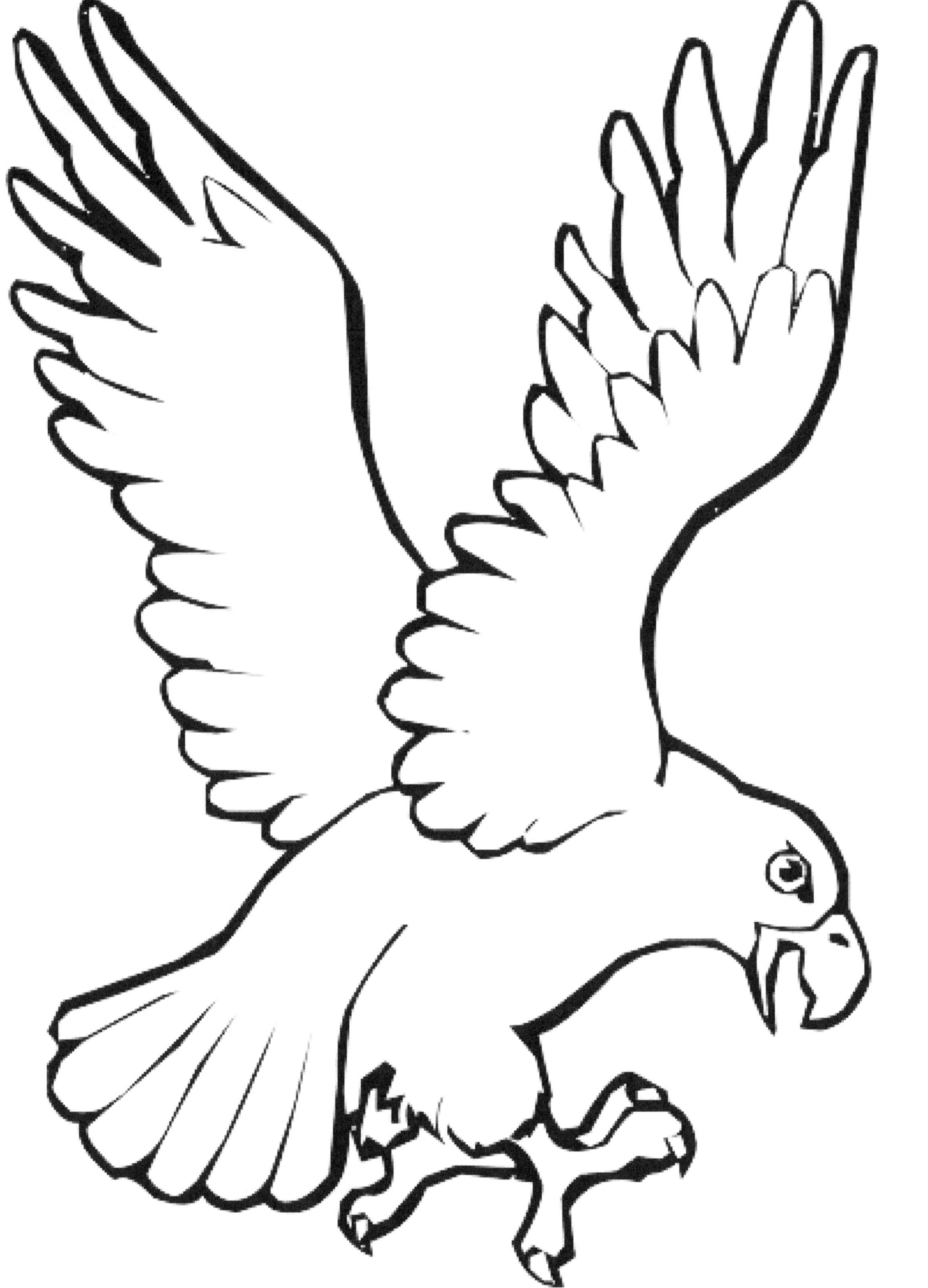

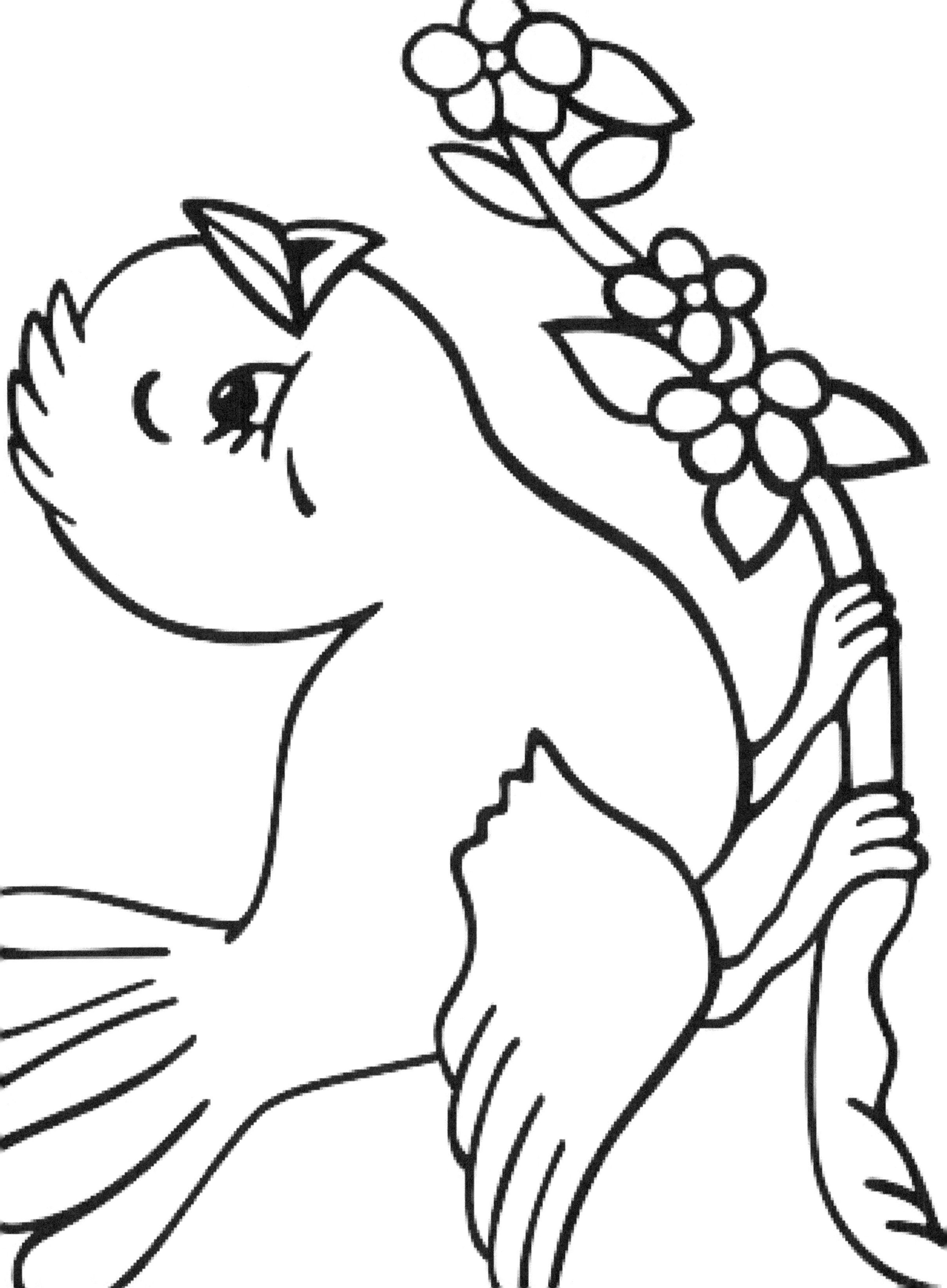

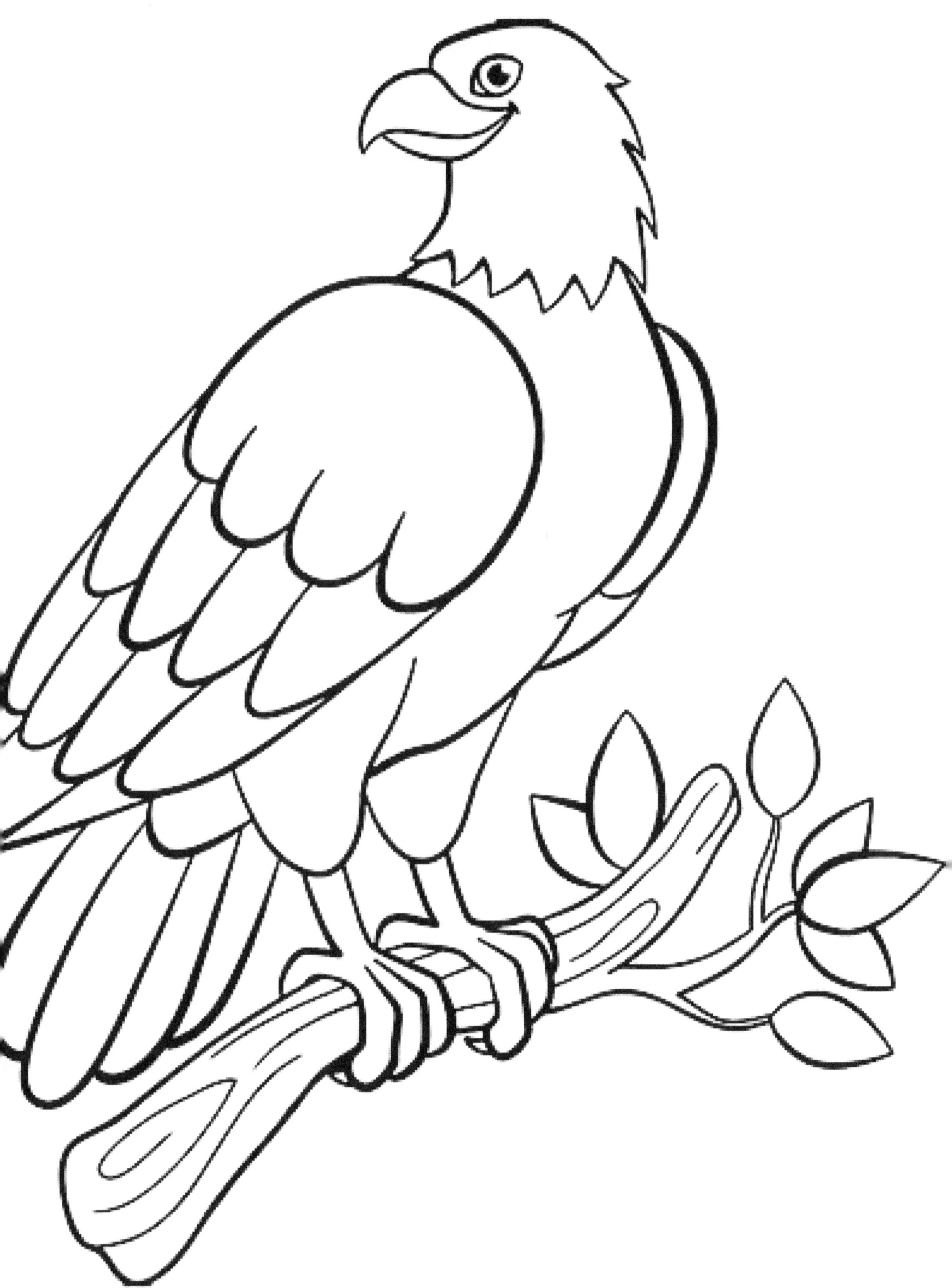

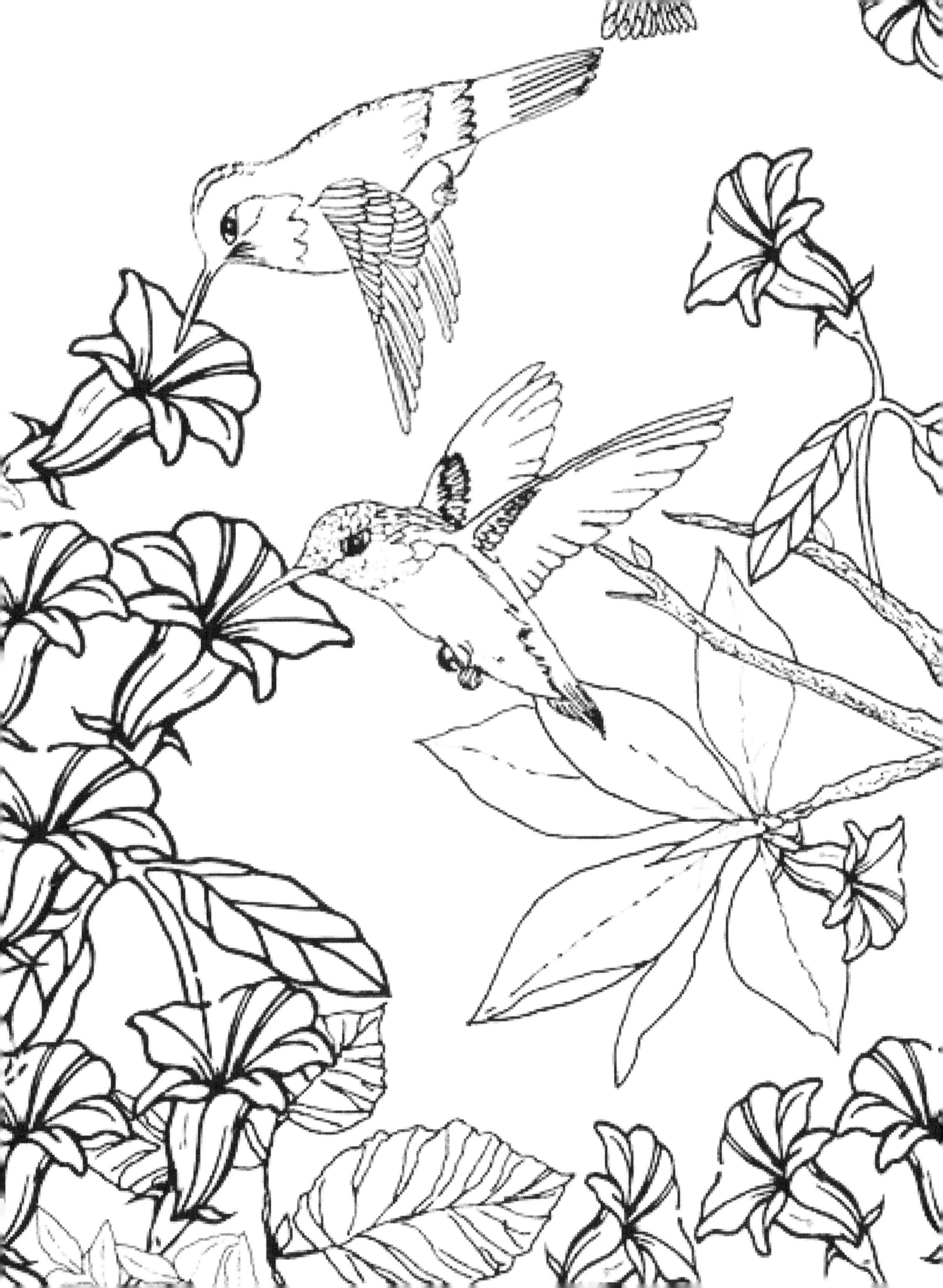

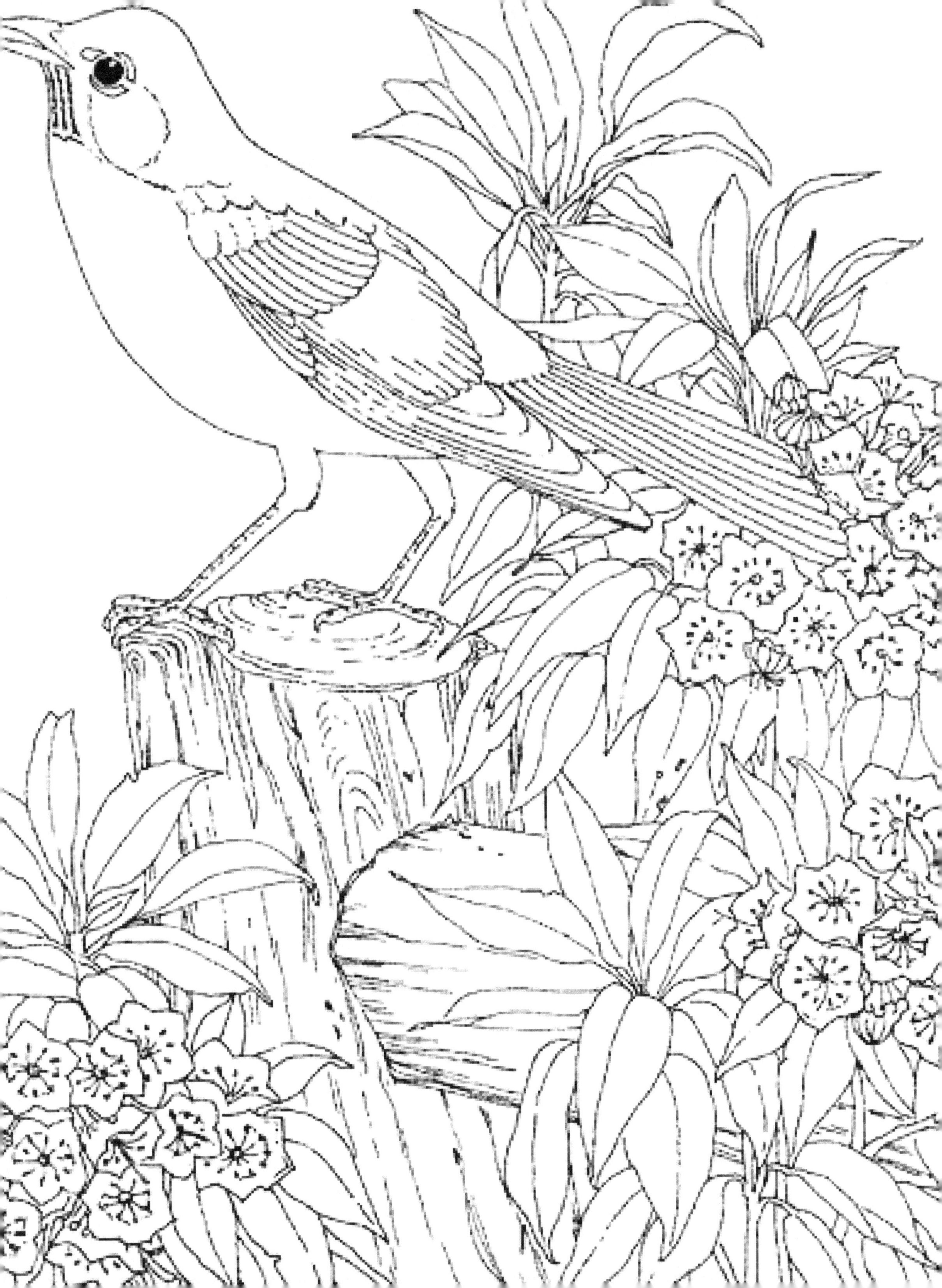

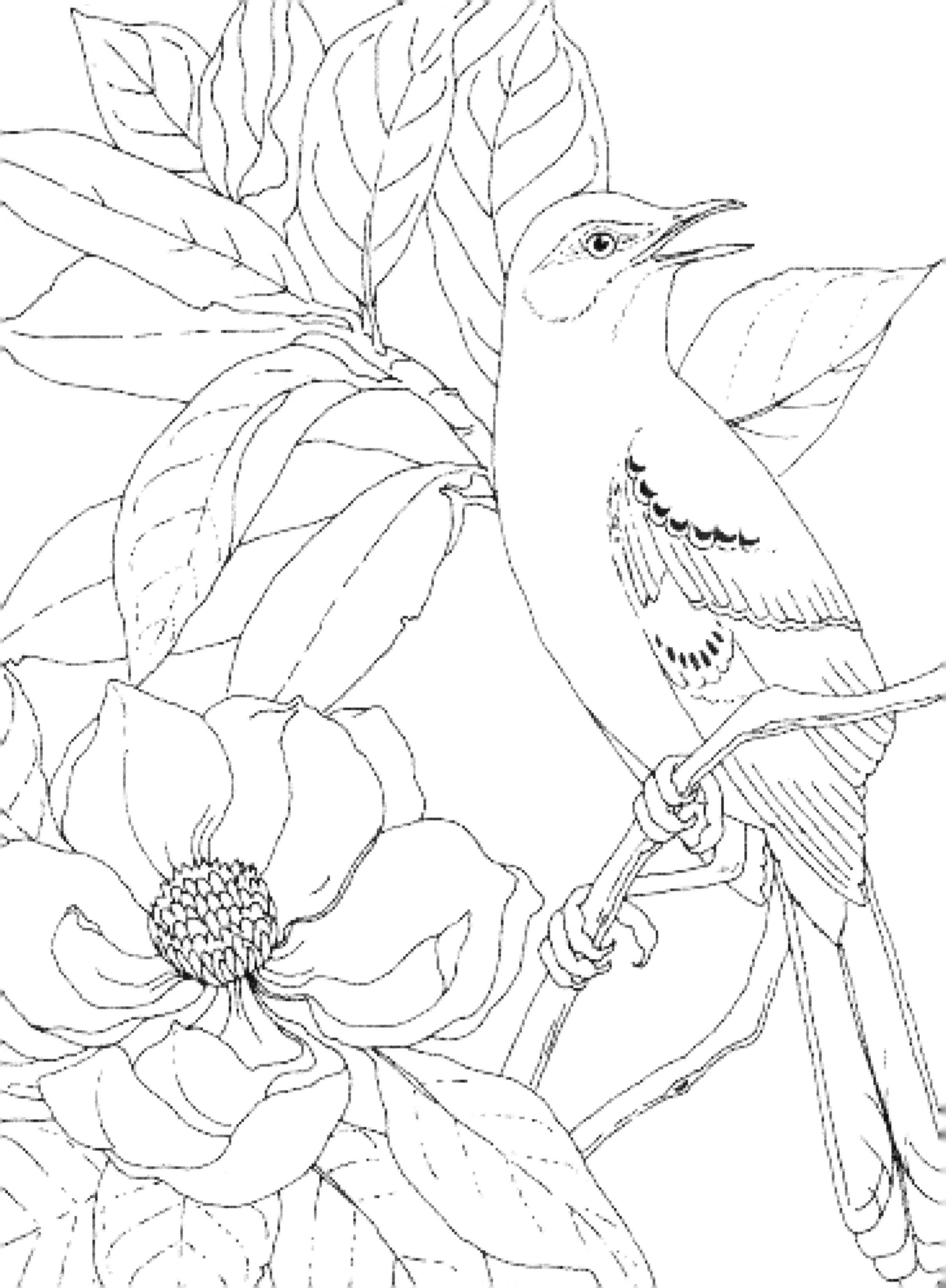

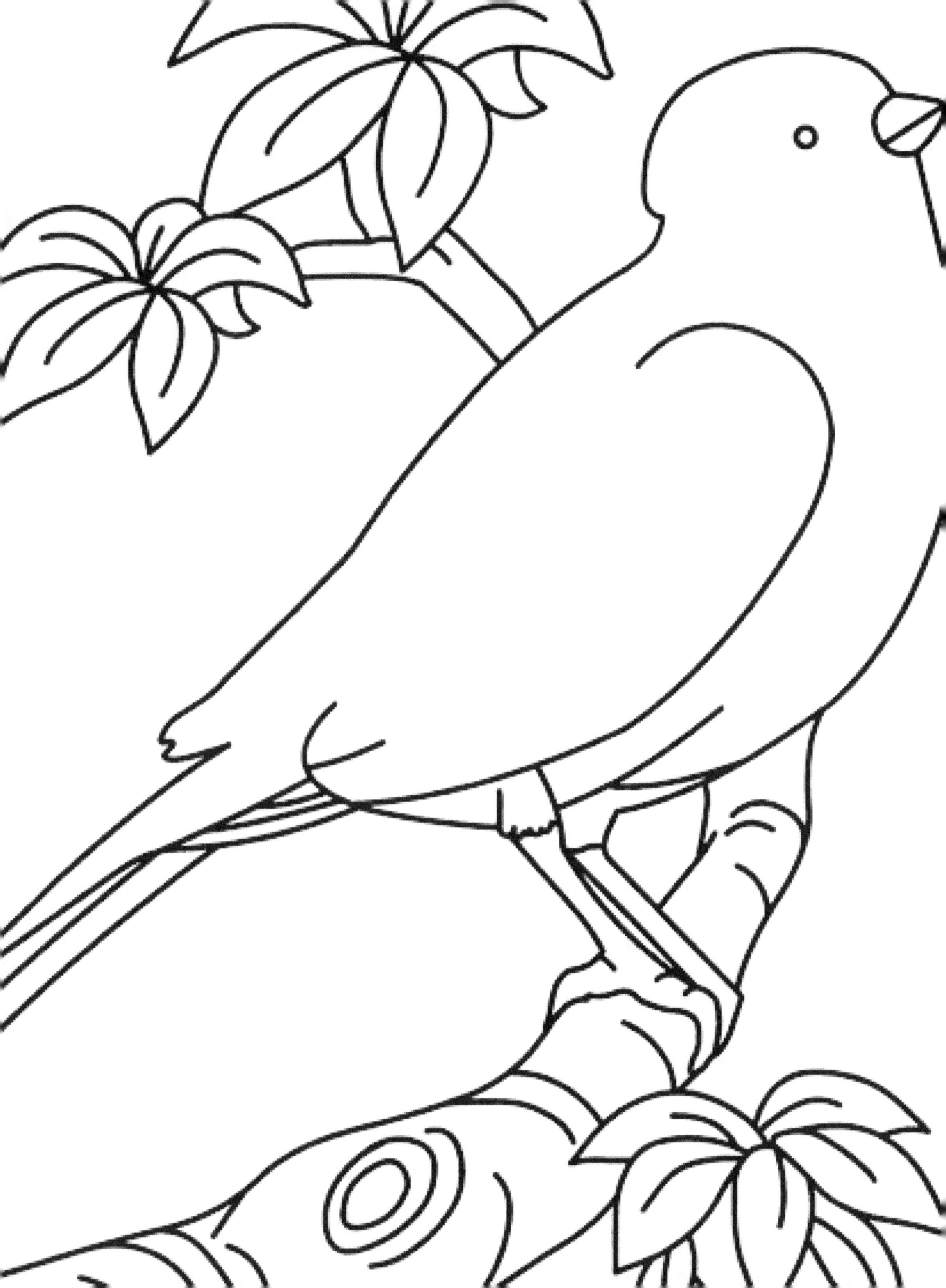

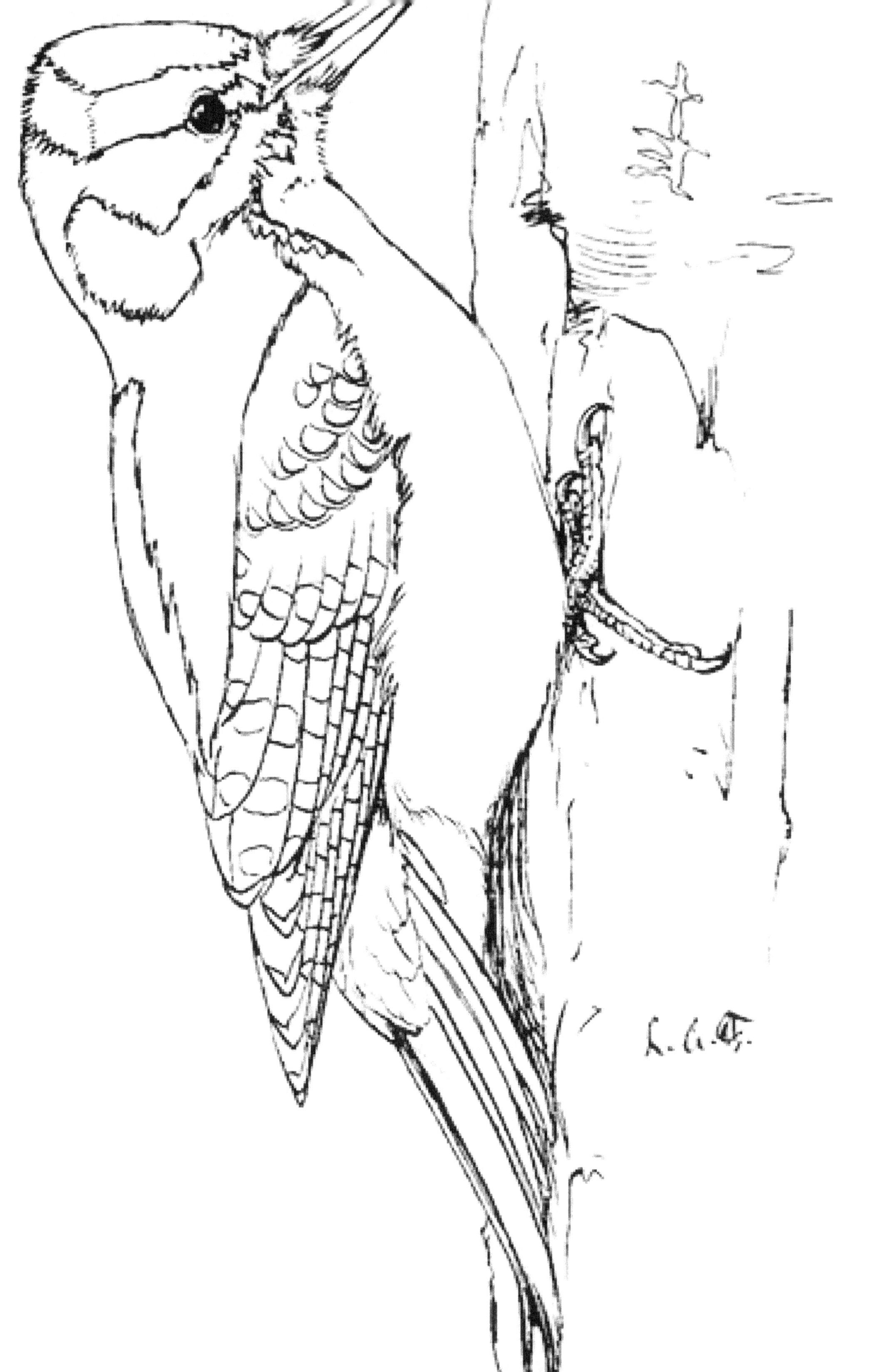

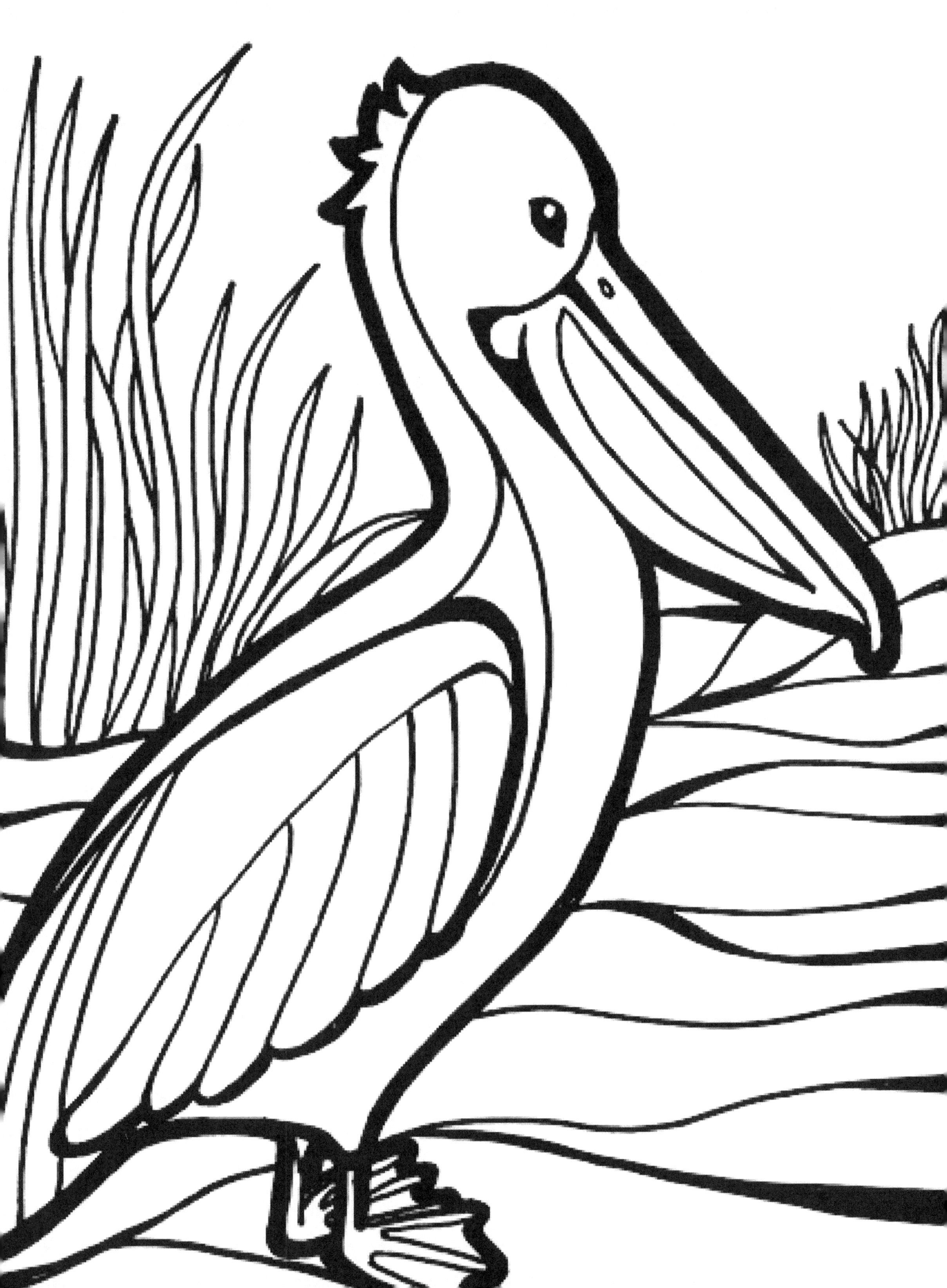

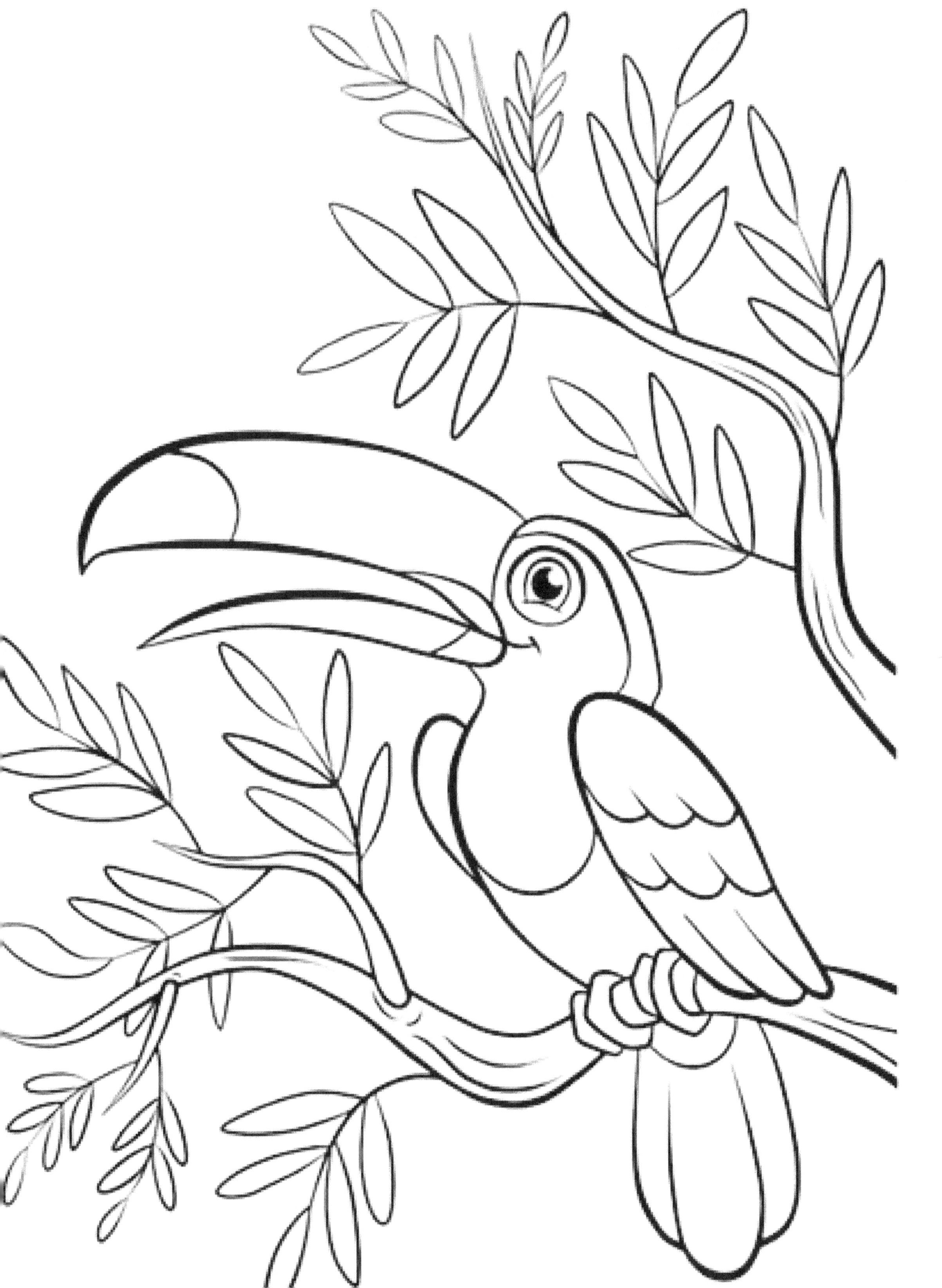

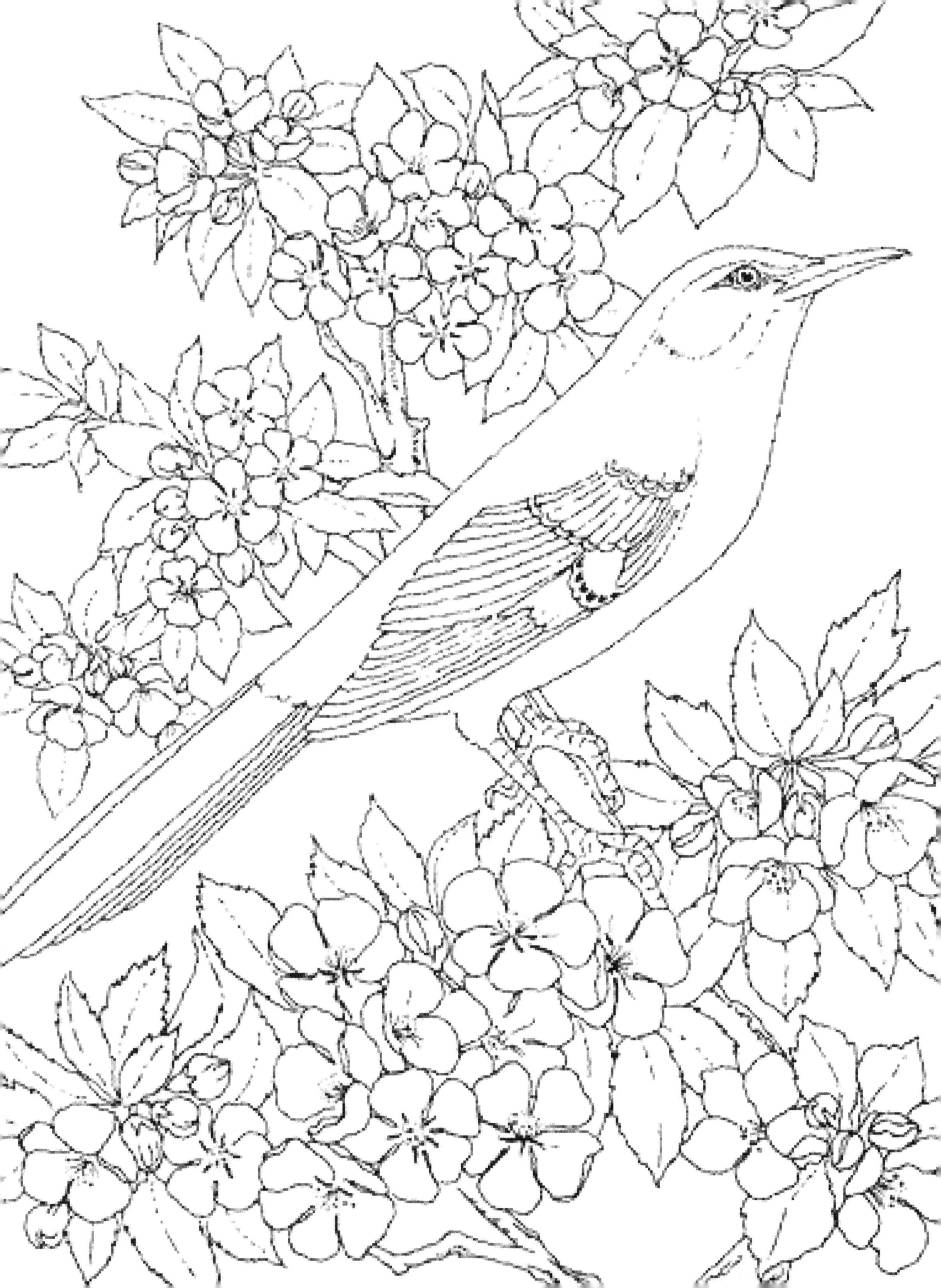

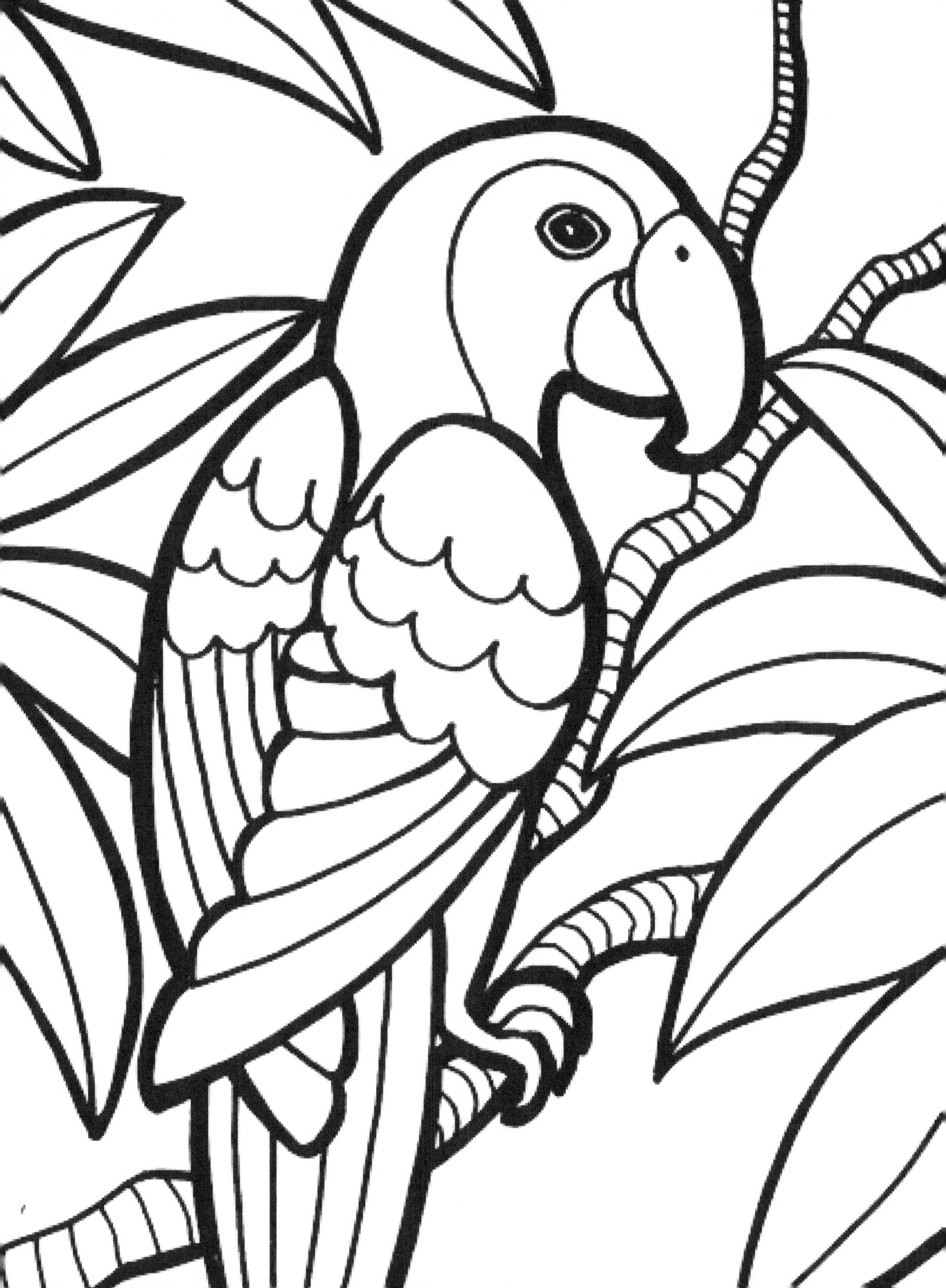

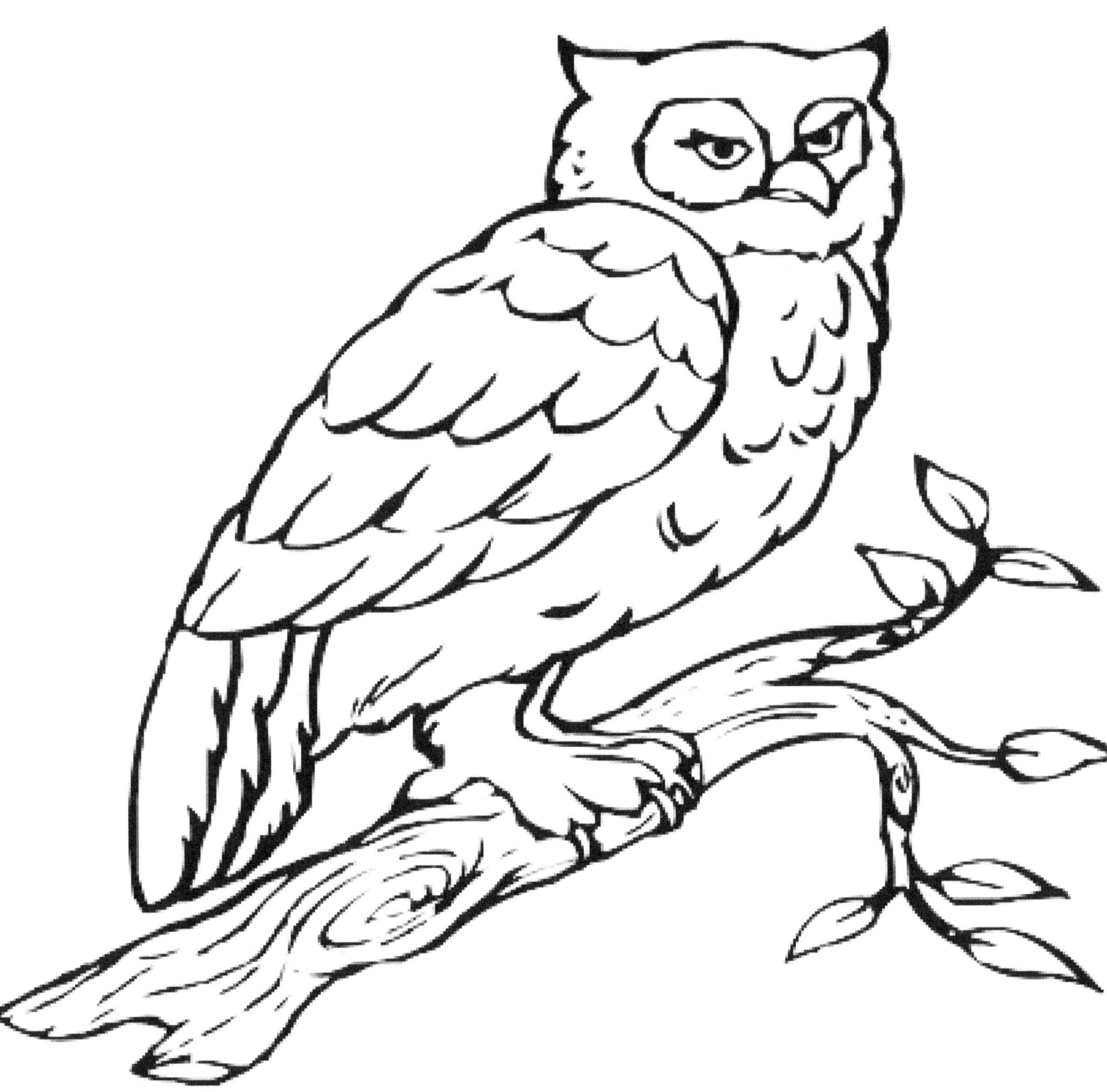

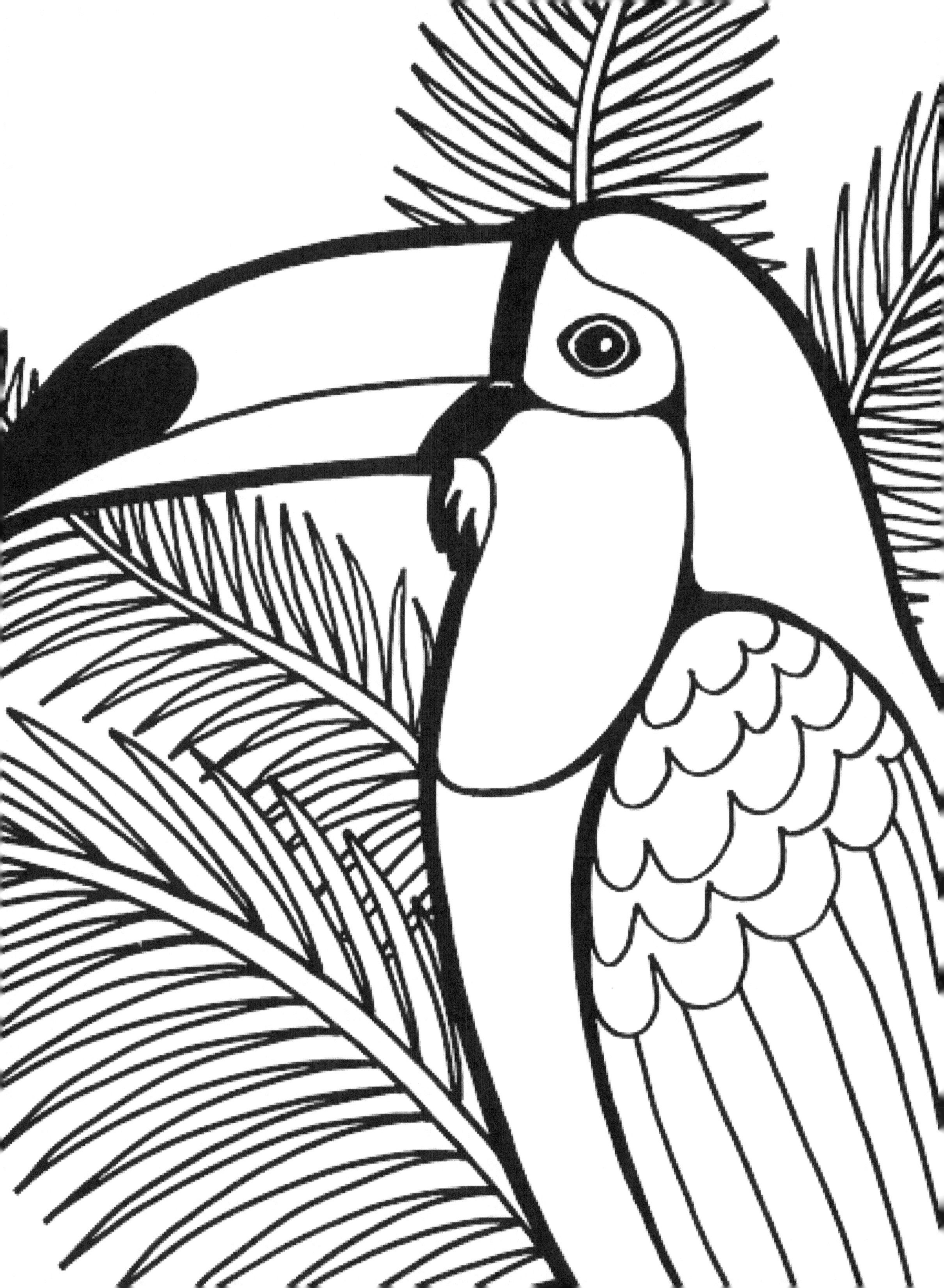

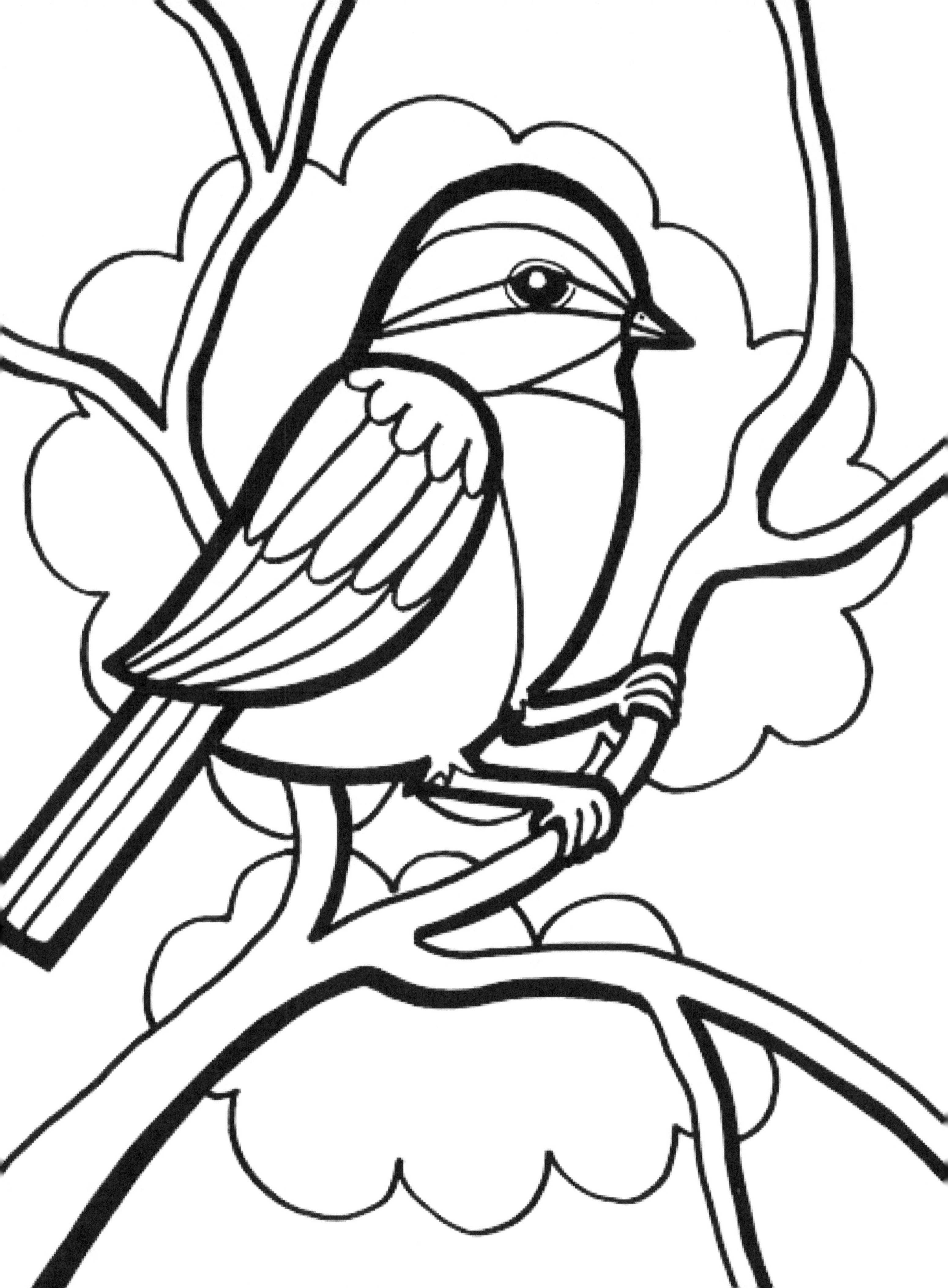

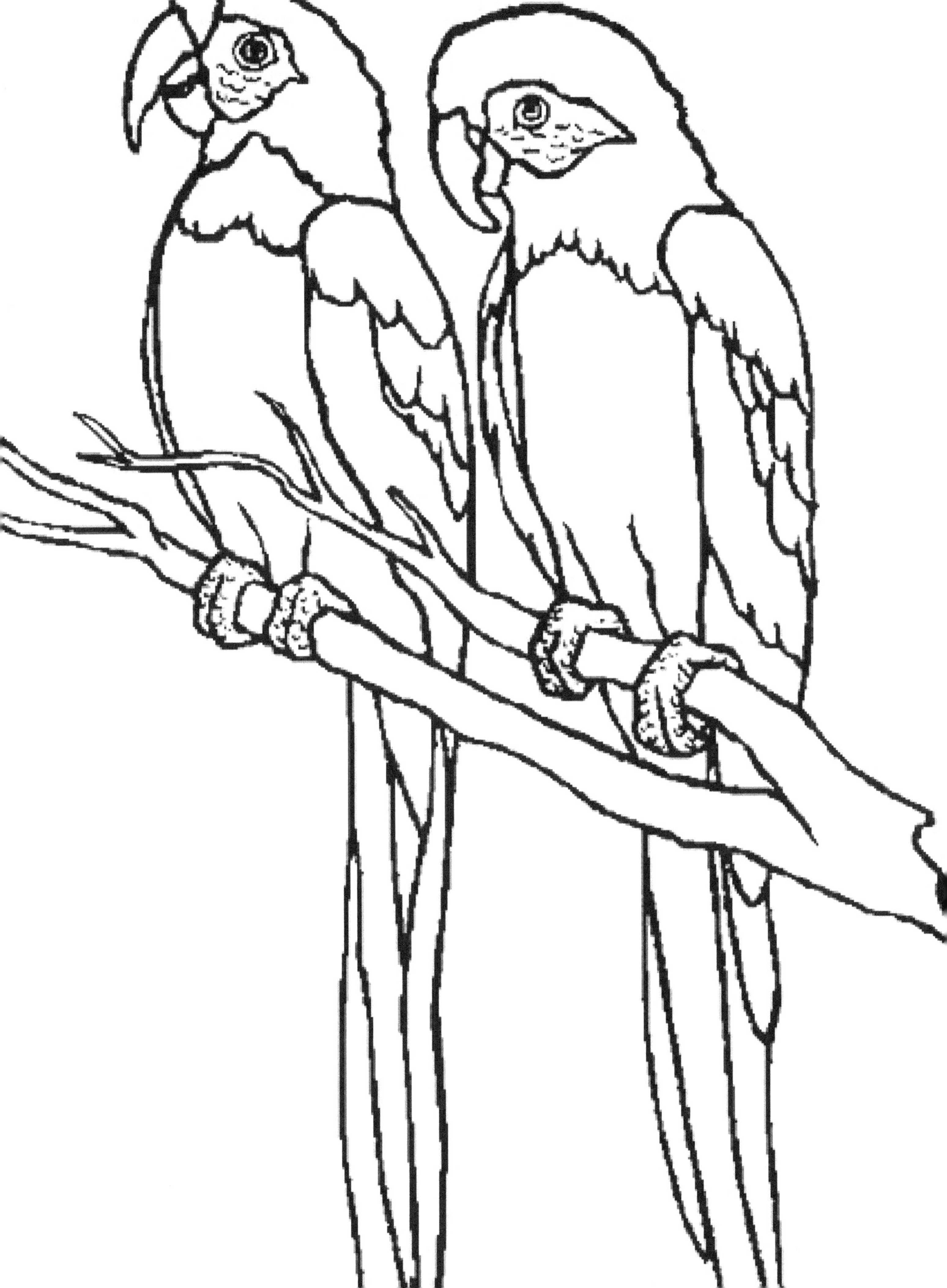